5 STEPS TO A

500

AP Macroeconomics
Questions

to know by test day

Also in the 5 Steps series:
5 Steps to a 5: AP Macroeconomics 2021
5 Steps to a 5: AP Macroeconomics 2021 Elite Student Edition
5 Steps to a 5: AP Microeconomics 2021
5 Steps to a 5: AP Microeconomics 2021 Elite Student Edition
5 Steps to a 5: AP Microeconomics/Macroeconomics Flashcards

Also in the 500 AP Questions to Know by Test Day series:
5 Steps to a 5: 500 AP Biology Questions to Know by Test Day, Third Edition
5 Steps to a 5: 500 AP Calculus AB/BC Questions to Know by Test Day Third Edition
5 Steps to a 5: 500 AP Chemistry Questions to Know by Test Day, Third Edition
5 Steps to a 5: 500 AP English Language Questions to Know by Test Day, Third Edition
5 Steps to a 5: 500 AP English Literature Questions to Know by Test Day Third Edition
5 Steps to a 5: 500 AP Environmental Science Questions to Know by Test Day, Third Edition
5 Steps to a 5: 500 AP European History Questions to Know by Test Day, Third Edition
5 Steps to a 5: 500 AP Human Geography to Know by Test Day, Third Edition
5 Steps to a 5: 500 AP Microeconomics Questions to Know by Test Day, Third Edition
5 Steps to a 5: 500 AP Physics 1 Questions to Know by Test Day, Third Edition
5 Steps to a 5: 500 AP Physics C Questions to Know by Test Day
5 Steps to a 5: 500 AP Psychology Questions to Know by Test Day, Third Edition
5 Steps to a 5: 500 AP Statistics Questions to Know by Test Day, Third Edition
5 Steps to a 5: 500 AP U.S. Government & Politics Questions to Know by Test Day, Second Edition
5 Steps to a 5: 500 AP U.S. History Questions to Know by Test Day, Third Edition
5 Steps to a 5: 500 AP World History Questions to Know by Test Day, Third Edition

5 STEPS TO A >

5™

500
AP Macroeconomics
Questions

to know by test day

THIRD EDITION

Anaxos, Inc.
Brian Reddington

New York Chicago San Francisco Athens London Madrid
Mexico City Milan New Delhi Singapore Sydney Toronto

CONTENTS

INTRODUCTION

Congratulations! You've taken a big step toward AP success by purchasing *5 Steps to a 5: 500 AP Macroeconomics Questions to Know by Test Day*. We are here to help you take the next step and score high on your AP exam so you can earn college credits and get into the college or university of your choice.

This book gives you 500 AP-style multiple-choice questions that cover all the most essential course material. Each question has a detailed answer explanation. These questions will give you valuable independent practice to supplement your regular textbook and the groundwork you are already doing in your AP classroom. This and the other books in this series were written by expert AP teachers who know your exam inside out and can identify the crucial exam information as well as questions that are most likely to appear on the exam.

You might be the kind of student who takes several AP courses and needs to study extra questions a few weeks before the exam for a final review. Or you might be the kind of student who puts off preparing until the last weeks before the exam. No matter what your preparation style, you will surely benefit from reviewing these 500 questions, which closely parallel the content, format, and degree of difficulty of the questions on the actual AP exam. These questions and their answer explanations are the ideal last-minute study tool for those final few weeks before the test.

Remember the old saying "Practice makes perfect." If you practice with all the questions and answers in this book, we are certain you will build the skills and confidence you need to do great on the exam. Good luck!

—*Editors of McGraw-Hill Education*

Diagnostic Quiz

GETTING STARTED: THE DIAGNOSTIC QUIZ

The following questions refer to different units in this book. These questions will help you test your understanding of the concepts tested on the AP exam by giving you an idea of where you need to focus your attention as you prepare. For each question, simply circle the letter of your choice. Once you are done with the exam, check your work against the given answers, which also indicate where you can find the corresponding material in the book.

Good luck!

DIAGNOSTIC QUIZ QUESTIONS

1. The local government increases its minimum wage requirement by $0.15. This will initially cause a change in the market for tacos in your area to change in what way?

   (A) Supply for tacos would increase.
   (B) Demand for tacos would increase.
   (C) Supply of tacos would decrease. *labor increase*
   (D) Both supply and demand for tacos would increase.
   (E) There would be no change in the market for tacos.

2. A decrease in the number of buyers and a technology increase will cause which of the following to occur?

   (A) Demand to increase and supply to remain unchanged.
   (B) Demand to decrease and supply to increase.
   (C) Both demand and supply to decrease.
   (D) Demand to increase and supply to decrease.
   (E) Both demand and supply to increase.

3. Being unemployed is defined by the government as

   (A) not having a job but actively seeking employment
   (B) not having a job
   (C) being employed part-time
   (D) not having a job but wanting one
   (E) being underemployed

Population	150,000
Employed	90,000
Unemployed	5,000
Discouraged Workers	2,500

4. Using the data provided, calculate the current unemployment rate.

   (A) 4.7 percent
   (B) 3.6 percent
   (C) 7 percent
   (D) 5.2 percent
   (E) 3 percent

$$\frac{unemployed}{labor\ force} \cdot 100\%$$

5. Using the data provided, calculate the labor force participation rate.
   (A) 72 percent
   (B) 63 percent
   (C) 60 percent
   (D) 65 percent
   (E) 67 percent

6. Using the data provided, calculate the labor force.
   (A) 85,000
   (B) 97,500
   (C) 55,000
   (D) 155,000
   (E) 95,000

7. If the full employment level of GDP for the economy is $500,000 and the current GDP of the economy is $540,000, the economy is experiencing a/an _____ and, with no government intervention, will adjust in the long run through what mechanism?
   (A) negative output gap; decrease in technology
   (B) equilibrium; increase in technology
   (C) inflationary gap; increase in wages
   (D) recessionary gap; increase in wages
   (E) positive output gap; decrease in wages

8. The long-run aggregate supply curve is representative of what value?
   (A) nominal GDP
   (B) current unemployment
   (C) equilibrium
   (D) the full employment output level of real GDP
   (E) current level of real GDP

9. When fluctuations in the aggregate price level have no effect on GDP, the economy is considered to be in what state?
   (A) depression
   (B) a recessionary gap
   (C) an inflationary gap
   (D) equilibrium
   (E) the long run

10. The relationship between savers and borrowers can be seen in which market?

    (A) money market
    (B) loanable funds market
    (C) foreign exchange market
    (D) aggregate supply/aggregate demand
    (E) banking market

11. To combat a recession, the government enacts policies that move the federal budget toward a deficit. How will this action affect the loanable funds market, the real interest rate, and gross private domestic investment?

	Loanable Funds	Interest Rate	Investment
(A)	supply increases	declines	decreases
(B)	demand increases	declines	increases
(C)	supply decreases	increases	increases
(D)	demand increases	increases	decreases
(E)	demand decreases	declines	decreases

12. Assume the economy is currently in a recessionary gap. What monetary policy would the central bank enact in order to correct the recession?

    (A) Sell bonds.
    (B) Raise the discount rate.
    (C) Buy bonds.
    (D) Decrease the money supply.
    (E) Decrease taxes.

13. The money supply curve is vertical because

    (A) Congress establishes the supply of money
    (B) the interest rate does not change
    (C) banks only lend to citizens in their own country
    (D) the central bank has monopoly control over the money supply
    (E) it is dependent on the interest rate to determine the quantity of money

14. The quantity theory of money is represented by what equation?
    (A) MV = PY
    (B) C + I + G + (X − M) = Y
    (C) MS = MD
    (D) PQ = MD
    (E) AD = AS

15. Economic growth can be represented by which of the following?
    (A) movement of the production possibilities curve to the left
    (B) movement of the short-run Phillips curve to the left
    (C) movement of the aggregate demand curve to the right
    (D) movement of long-run aggregate supply to the right
    (E) movement of long-run aggregate supply to the left

16. When the government moves its budget toward a deficit, it needs to borrow to cover the deficit. How would this impact the loanable funds market?
    (A) Both supply and demand increase, interest rates rise, and investment is crowded out.
    (B) Demand increases, interest rates fall, and investment is crowded in.
    (C) Supply increases, interest rates rise, and investment is crowded in.
    (D) Supply decreases, interest rates fall, and investment is crowded out.
    (E) Demand increases, interest rates rise, and investment is crowded out.

17. What combination of fiscal and monetary policy would most likely increase GDP?
    (A) Increase taxes and sell bonds.
    (B) Decrease taxes and buy bonds.
    (C) Decrease taxes and sell bonds.
    (D) Increase spending and interest rates.
    (E) Decrease spending and interest rates.

18. How is the government's budget surplus calculated?

    (A) The government can never run a surplus.
    (B) (government spending – taxes) + foreign assets
    (C) tax revenues – (government spending + transfer payments)
    (D) tax revenues + government spending + transfer payments
    (E) tax revenues – (government spending – transfer payments)

19. If the economy of a foreign nation is experiencing a high rate of growth in relation to the home country's economy, what effect will this have on the equilibrium exchange rate for the home country's currency?

    (A) It will appreciate.
    (B) It will depreciate.
    (C) It will remain unchanged.
    (D) It will only affect the foreign nations exchange rate.
    (E) It will cause inflation.

20. Net exports (X – M), net income from abroad and net unilateral transfers, are part of what sector of the economy?

    (A) the bond market
    (B) the current account
    (C) the open market
    (D) the government's budget
    (E) the capital financial account

DIAGNOSTIC QUIZ ANSWERS

1. (Chapter 1: Basic Economic Concepts)

ANSWER: (C) The minimum wage increase would be an increase in input prices (labor) for the production of tacos. Therefore, the supply of tacos would decrease.

2. (Chapter 1: Basic Economic Concepts)

ANSWER: (B) The numbers of buyers decreasing is a determinant of demand for the item, causing demand to decrease at all prices or a shift to the left of the demand curve. An increase in the technology for the product is an increase in the determinant of supply, causing supply to increase at all prices or a shift to the right of the supply curve.

3. (Chapter 2: Economic Indicators and the Business Cycle)

ANSWER: (A) The current economic definition of unemployment is that the individual does not currently have a job and is actively seeking employment.

4. (Chapter 2: Economic Indicators and the Business Cycle)

ANSWER: (D) The unemployment rate is calculated as the number of unemployed divided by the labor force multiplied by 100. 5,000 (unemployed)/95,000 (unemployed + employed) × 100 = 5.2%.

5. (Chapter 2: Economic Indicators and the Business Cycle)

ANSWER: (B) The labor force participation rate is calculated as the total labor force divided by the total population multiplied by 100. (95,000 (employed + unemployed)/150,000) × 100 = 63%.

6. (Chapter 2: Economic Indicators and the Business Cycle)

ANSWER: (E) The labor force is calculated as the number of unemployed added to the number of employed. 5,000 + 90,000 = 95,000.

7. (Chapter 3: National Income and Price Determination)

ANSWER: (C) In this economy, there is a $40,000 positive output gap, commonly known as an inflationary gap. If no government intervention takes place, wages in the labor market will increase as workers will request higher wages to offset the increased inflation. This will cause a decrease in aggregate supply, moving the economy back to long-run full employment equilibrium output.

8. (Chapter 3: National Income and Price Determination)

ANSWER: (D) Long-run aggregate supply is vertical at the full employment level of real GDP and represents the level of production necessary to reach full employment within an economy, as well as the point at which the relationship between prices and wages are fully flexible.

9. (Chapter 3: National Income and Price Determination)

ANSWER: (E) The long-run aggregate supply (LRAS) curve is vertical at the full employment rate of real GDP. This means that any change in the aggregate price level will simply move up and down the LRAS without changing the level of real output.

10. (Chapter 4: The Financial Sector)

ANSWER: (B) The supply of loanable funds (SLF) comes from the actions of savers, and the demand for loanable funds (DLF) comes from borrowers. Therefore, the loanable funds market brings these two groups together to establish the real interest rate at the equilibrium point of SLF and DLF.

11. (Chapter 4: The Financial Sector)

ANSWER: (D) When the government moves its budget toward a deficit, it must borrow from the loanable funds market to cover that deficit. This causes the demand for loanable funds (DLF) to increase. As DLF moves to the right, interest rates rise, causing the cost of investing to rise and total investment to decrease. This is known as the "crowding out" of investment.

12. (Chapter 4: The Financial Sector)

ANSWER: (C) When the central bank buys bonds, the process increases the money supply. The increase in the money supply will lower interest rates, which increases interest-sensitive investment and consumption. This will move aggregate demand to the right, increasing gross domestic product and decreasing the recession.

13. (Chapter 4: The Financial Sector)

ANSWER: (D) The central bank of a country has sole control of the money supply. They determine the interest rates by manipulating the supply of money, otherwise known as monetary policy.

14. (Chapter 5: Long-Run Consequences of Stabilization Policies)

ANSWER: (A) M is the supply of money, V is the velocity of money, P is the price level, and Y is GDP. This formula is used by monetarists to justify some monetary policy actions.

15. (Chapter 5: Long-Run Consequences of Stabilization Policies)

ANSWER: (D) An increase in long-run aggregate supply is shown by its movement to the right, which represents an increase in the potential output of the economy, also known as growth.

16. (Chapter 5: Long-Run Consequences of Stabilization Policies)

ANSWER: (E) When the government moves its budget toward a deficit, it must borrow from the loanable funds market, causing either the supply to move to the left or the demand to move to the right. Either movement will cause the interest rate to rise, which causes the cost of investment to rise, which crowds out investment.

17. (Chapter 5: Long-Run Consequences of Stabilization Policies)

ANSWER: (B) Decreasing taxes will increase the amount of disposable income, causing consumption to increase. Buying bonds increases the money supply, which lowers the interest rate, causing investment to increase. Both of these actions lead to an increase to aggregate demand, leading to an increase in GDP.

18. (Chapter 5: Long-Run Consequences of Stabilization Policies)

ANSWER: (C) To calculate any budget deficit or surplus, you must subtract any government expenditures (spending and transfer payments) from the amount of tax revenue received in a given year.

19. (Chapter 6: Open Economy—International Trade and Finance)

ANSWER: (A) The foreign country's growth will increase demand for more foreign goods from the home country. This will increase the demand for the home country's currency, causing its currency to appreciate.

20. (Chapter 6: Open Economy—International Trade and Finance)

ANSWER: (B) All of the components listed are part of the current account. This is the interaction of countries in the exchange of goods and services across borders.

CHAPTER 1

Basic Economic Concepts

1. Macroeconomics is defined as the concentration and analysis of
   (A) the overall ups and downs of the economy
   (B) individuals and firms
   (C) specific industries within the economy
   (D) normative and positive economic theories
   (E) the scarcity of resources for industry

Refer to the following diagram to answer question 2.

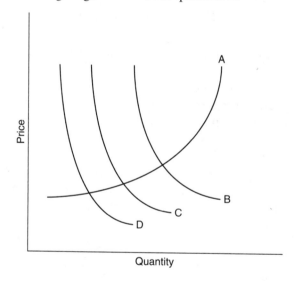

2. According to the preceding diagram, the relationship between price and quantity supplied is illustrated by which line?

   (A) A
   (B) B
   (C) C
   (D) D
   (E) A and B

3. When are specialization and gains from trade beneficial?

   (A) only when a tariff is collected
   (B) when the standard of living within a country increases
   (C) when inflation decreases
   (D) never, as trade causes unemployment
   (E) if a country gains resources at the expense of the other country

4. A country is said to have a comparative advantage over another country when which of the following occurs?

   (A) It can produce a good at a lower opportunity cost than another country.
   (B) It can produce a good utilizing fewer resources per unit of output than another country.
   (C) There is a higher degree of specialization and division of labor compared with another country's.
   (D) When comparing each country's production possibilities frontiers, one country is operating at maximum efficiency and output.
   (E) One country's production possibilities frontier is shifted further to the right compared with another country's production possibilities frontier.

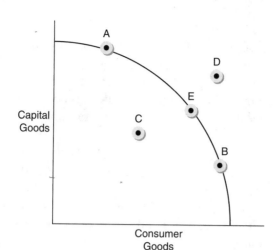

5. Using the preceding production possibilities curve, the economy can operate at point D if they
   (A) decrease the production of one good
   (B) decrease unemployment
   (C) engage in specialization and trade
   (D) increase the production of one good
   (E) move production from one good to the other

6. It is beneficial for two countries to trade only when there is/are
   (A) a mutually beneficial trade agreement
   (B) increasing returns to scale
   (C) decreasing returns to scale
   (D) an absolute advantage in production between the two countries
   (E) a comparative advantage in production between the two countries

7. Any point along the production possibilities curve is
   (A) attainable and efficient
   (B) attainable yet inefficient
   (C) unattainable and inefficient
   (D) showing that resources are not being utilized to their full potential
   (E) none of the above

8. What does economic growth refer to?
   (A) a rightward shift of the production possibilities curve
   (B) movement along the demand curve
   (C) movement along the supply curve
   (D) the point where the supply and demand curves intersect
   (E) the allocation of private property into public sectors

9. The production possibilities curve is concave because
   (A) as production of goods and services increases, the opportunity costs decrease
   (B) taxes increase as the production of a good increases
   (C) as production of goods and services increases, the opportunity costs increase
   (D) both B and C
   (E) both A and C

10. Tommy has two free hours to do whatever he would like. He thinks of the many activities he might engage in and settles on a choice between tutoring his younger brother in AP Economics or sitting and watching television. His parents pay him $10 per hour when he helps his brother study. He chooses to sit and watch television for two hours. What is the opportunity cost of this decision?
    (A) $20, because opportunity cost is the next best alternative given up when a decision is made
    (B) $0, because the marginal benefit is greater than the marginal cost of watching television
    (C) $10, because the marginal benefit is greater than the marginal cost of watching television
    (D) $0, because the opportunity cost is the next best alternative given up when a decision is made
    (E) none of the above

11. Your school decides to build a new performing arts center. What is the opportunity cost of constructing the new performing arts center?
    (A) the money used for the construction of the performing arts center
    (B) the cost of building the performing arts center now, rather than waiting until next year
    (C) any other good or service that now cannot be provided due to the resources used for the new performing arts center
    (D) without the knowledge of the next best option for using the resources that went to the performing arts center, the answer cannot be known
    (E) none of the above

12. Both of the economies of the fictional nations Reilly and Tanen have the same production possibilities curve. They both are operating at the same point on the curve. If Tanen discovers a new resource for production, the most likely result of the production possibilities curves would be
    (A) Tanen's curve would shift to the right, whereas Reilly's would stay the same
    (B) both Tanen's and Reilly's curves would shift to the right
    (C) Tanen's curve would shift to the right, whereas Reilly's would shift to the left
    (D) Tanen's curve would stay the same, whereas Reilly's would shift to the left
    (E) none of the above

13. If resources are overallocated in a market, then
    (A) consumer spending would increase due to an increase in demand
    (B) quantity supplied would be less than the allocatively efficient quantity
    (C) the opportunity cost of producing one more unit would increase exponentially
    (D) quantity supplied would be more than the allocatively efficient quantity
    (E) quantity supplied would be equal to the allocatively efficient quantity

14. All of the following are examples of a market economy EXCEPT
    (A) competition among sellers of products
    (B) government ownership of the factors of production
    (C) freedom of sellers to enter and exit the market
    (D) unrestricted consumer choice
    (E) the existence of markets

15. The boundary between attainable and unattainable outputs is represented by which of the following?
    (A) the Laffer curve
    (B) the Phillips curve
    (C) the equilibrium point between supply and demand
    (D) the point of diminishing returns
    (E) the production possibilities curve

16. *Scarcity* is best defined as
    (A) material resources that are limited
    (B) an idea used by industrializing nations to satisfy unlimited wants and desires with limited natural resources
    (C) limited vital material resources compared with limited wants and needs
    (D) all points lying outside the production possibilities curve
    (E) the idea that a society's wants and needs are unlimited, and material resources are limited

17. Both Luca and Sarah can weed the garden and walk their dog on Sunday morning. For every half hour of walking the dog, Luca can weed twice the amount of garden Sarah can. According to this information,
    (A) Sarah walks the dog because she has absolute advantage in weeding the garden
    (B) Luca walks the dog because he has comparative advantage in weeding the garden
    (C) Luca weeds the garden because he has comparative advantage in weeding the garden
    (D) Sarah weeds the garden because she has comparative advantage in weeding the garden
    (E) Sarah walks the dog because she has comparative advantage in walking the dog

absolute: produce more
comparative: -''- with less opportunity cost

18. If the current market price for a product is higher than the equilibrium market price, it will cause the market to adjust in which way?

(A) There would be upward pressure on the market price due to the deficit in the market.

(B) There would be upward pressure on the market price due to the surplus in the market.

(C) There would be downward pressure on the market price due to the deficit in the market.

(D) There would be downward pressure on the market price due to the surplus in the market.

(E) There would be no change in the price or quantity within the market.

19. What is the significant difference between quantity supplied and aggregate supply?

(A) Quantity supplied is the total amount of a good that is available to consumers; aggregate supply is the total supply of goods in an economy.

(B) Quantity supplied is the total supply of goods available in an economy; aggregate supply is the total amount of a good available to consumers.

(C) Quantity supplied is the total amount of a good that is available to consumers; aggregate supply is the total amount of goods demanded and supplied in an economy.

(D) Quantity supplied is the total amount of a good demanded by consumers; aggregate supply is the total amount of goods demanded and supplied by producers.

(E) none of the above

20. Mineral deposits, human capital, entrepreneurship, use of technology, and machinery are all examples of which of the following?

(A) factors of production

(B) superior and inferior goods

(C) elements sometimes needed to move an existing company overseas

(D) public goods

(E) material wants and needs

21. Which of the following will cause an outward shift of the production possibilities curve?
    (A) cuts in funding in educational training for employees
    (B) a decrease in a nation's birthrate, thus decreasing the labor force
    (C) a natural disaster creating extreme limitations of a vital natural resource
    (D) an increase in skilled workers
    (E) none of the above

22. The term *ceteris paribus* means
    (A) if event A precedes event B, A caused B
    (B) economics deals with facts, not values
    (C) other things equal
    (D) prosperity inevitably follows recession
    (E) out of many, one

23. How is it possible for a country to consume more than its production possibilities curve dictates?
    (A) not possible without greater quantities of the factors of production already obtained
    (B) specialization and trade
    (C) increase in education and job training
    (D) obtainment of a greater quantity of affordable substitutes
    (E) increase in the division of labor

24. The production possibilities curve will show a straight line if which of the following is true?
    (A) The opportunity cost is constant.
    (B) Vital resources for the good are limitless.
    (C) The economy is operating below maximum efficiency and output.
    (D) The law of decreasing marginal utility does not apply.
    (E) Marginal benefit is less than marginal cost.

25. According to the law of demand,
    (A) as the price of a good or service increases, the demand will shift to the right
    (B) as the price of a good or service increases, the demand will shift to the left
    (C) there is an inverse relationship between quantity demanded of a good or service and the price of that good or service
    (D) as prices for a good or service increase, consumers will begin to use complementary goods
    (E) as the price of a good or service increases, the quantity demanded will increase

26. Within the market system, prices are determined by which of the following?
    (A) supply and demand
    (B) a central planning committee
    (C) opportunity cost
    (D) aggregate demand
    (E) the Federal Reserve

27. Suppose a very dry and hot season contributes to a poor yield of cotton for the year. As a result, the low supply of cotton increases the cost of cotton T-shirts. How does this cause the market for shirts made of other fabrics to change?
    (A) The demand for shirts made of other fabrics will increase due to the higher price of its complement, cotton T-shirts.
    (B) The market for shirts made of other fabrics will not change.
    (C) The demand for shirts made of other fabrics will decrease due to the higher price of its complement, cotton T-shirts.
    (D) The supply for shirts made of other fabrics will increase due to the higher price of its substitute, cotton T-shirts.
    (E) The demand for shirts made of other fabrics will increase due to the higher price of its substitute, cotton T-shirts.

28. Both bowling balls and bowling shoes are necessary for bowling. If the demand for bowling balls increases, what could be said regarding bowling shoes?

    (A) The demand for bowling shoes will decrease.
    (B) The demand for bowling shoes will increase.
    (C) The price of bowling shoes will decrease.
    (D) The quantity supplied will decrease.
    (E) none of the above

29. Without government regulations, the equilibrium price is established

    (A) at the next price above where the demand and supply curves intersect
    (B) when the quantity supplied equals the quantity demanded
    (C) at the next price below where the demand and supply curves intersect
    (D) when you take the difference between the two lowest points plotted on the demand and supply curves
    (E) at the price where either the demand or supply curve becomes horizontal

30. Terms of trade are defined as

    (A) the rate at which one good can be exchanged for another internationally
    (B) the price of a currency in the foreign exchange market
    (C) the price of a good within an economy
    (D) the exchange rate of currency for products sold outside of an economy
    (E) resource prices within an economy

31. In the market for tacos, if more people move into town, the market will change in which way?
    (A) The supply of tacos will increase.
    (B) The demand for tacos will increase.
    (C) The demand for tacos will decrease.
    (D) The supply of tacos will decrease.
    (E) Both the supply and demand for tacos will decrease.

32. The increase or decrease of supply of a product is determined by all of the following EXCEPT
    (A) input prices
    (B) competition
    (C) income of consumers
    (D) expectations of price changes
    (E) government subsidies

33. A supply curve differs from a demand curve in that
    (A) it slopes upward while a demand curve slopes downward
    (B) it slopes downward while a demand curve slopes upward
    (C) it is longer than a demand curve
    (D) it is always vertical
    (E) it is always horizontal

34. Why would Greece trade with Russia?
    (A) to eliminate its deficit
    (B) to eliminate its surplus
    (C) if Russia eliminates tariffs
    (D) if the terms of trade were mutually beneficial
    (E) if Russia agrees to decrease the exchange rate

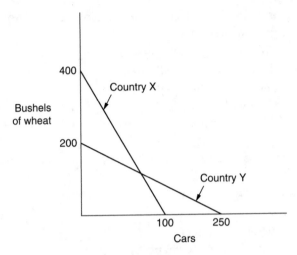

35. According to the preceding production possibilities frontier, what would be the minimum price country X will accept to export wheat to country Y?

    (A) 2 cars
    (B) 4 cars
    (C) 1 car
    (D) ½ car
    (E) ¼ car

$$\frac{100}{400} = \frac{1}{4} \text{ car}$$

36. When a country has a comparative advantage over another country

    (A) it can produce more of one good than the other country can
    (B) it can produce more of two goods than the other country can
    (C) international trade will benefit both countries
    (D) international trade will not benefit both countries
    (E) the other country should implement a trade embargo to protect its market

37. A point inside the production possibilities curve is

    (A) attainable and efficient
    (B) attainable yet inefficient
    (C) unattainable and efficient
    (D) unattainable and inefficient
    (E) only achievable through international trade

38. In a production possibilities graph, a recession is shown as a

 (A) point inside the curve
 (B) leftward shift of the production possibilities curve
 (C) rightward shift of the production possibilities curve
 (D) point on the production possibilities curve
 (E) point outside the production possibilities curve

39. What does a flat production possibilities curve represent?

 (A) increasing opportunity costs
 (B) decreasing opportunity costs
 (C) unspecialized resources
 (D) specialized resources
 (E) a shortage of resources

40. When a nation has specialized resources, its production possibilities curve will reflect

 (A) unchanging opportunity costs
 (B) increasing opportunity costs
 (C) decreasing opportunity costs
 (D) a shortage of labor
 (E) inefficient production

41. China decides to build an aircraft carrier. What is the opportunity cost of the aircraft carrier?

 (A) cash used to build the aircraft carrier
 (B) the cost of issuing bonds to pay for the aircraft carrier instead of paying cash
 (C) cannot be answered because an alternative use of resources was not provided
 (D) any other good or service that China cannot provide because of resources used to build the aircraft carrier
 (E) the annual cost of operating the aircraft carrier when construction is complete

42. A major oilfield in Saudi Arabia runs out of oil, a production resource. Meanwhile, oil production remains steady in Russia. What would the production possibilities curves for Saudi Arabia and Russia do, respectively?

    (A) shift to the right, shift to the left
    (B) shift to the right, remain the same
    (C) shift to the left, remain the same
    (D) shift to the left, shift to the right
    (E) remain the same, shift to the left

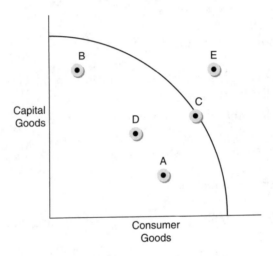

43. Use the preceding production possibilities curve. When labor within an economy is at full employment, the point within the production possibilities graph will be where?

    (A) Point A
    (B) Point B
    (C) Point C
    (D) Point D
    (E) Point E

Use the market for golf balls to answer questions 44 and 45.

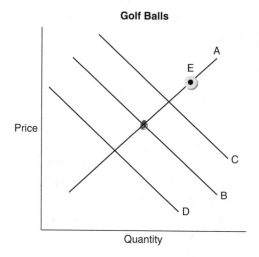

Golf Balls

44. Starting at the intersection of lines A and B, consider this question: If the price of a round of golf declines in your area, what effect will this have on the market for golf balls?

   (A) Demand will increase as shown by Line D.
   (B) Supply will increase as shown by Point E.
   (C) Demand will increase as shown by Line C.
   (D) Demand will decrease as shown by Line D.
   (E) The market for golf balls will not change.

45. Starting at the intersection of lines A and B, consider this question: If more people are taking up bowling than golf, what effect will this have on the market for golf balls?

   (A) Demand will increase as shown by Line D.
   (B) Supply will increase as shown by Point E.
   (C) Demand will increase as shown by Line C.
   (D) Demand will decrease as shown by Line D.
   (E) The market for golf balls will not change.

46. When a nation's output is located at a point on the production possibilities curve

   (A) it has high unemployment
   (B) it has moderate unemployment
   (C) it has full employment
   (D) it has low unemployment
   (E) it has underemployment

47. France decides to stop buying aircraft carriers from the United States, instead choosing to manufacture them itself. France's decision could be based on what economic concept?
    (A) unemployment
    (B) inflation
    (C) surplus
    (D) shortage
    (E) opportunity cost

48. If immigration increases the supply of labor in a country
    (A) the production possibilities curve will shift to the right
    (B) the production possibilities curve will shift to the left
    (C) the production possibilities curve will remain in the same place
    (D) output will move along the production possibilities curve
    (E) human capital will decrease

49. As a consequence of scarcity
    (A) producing more of one good means producing less of another good
    (B) producing more of one good can be accomplished without any sacrifices
    (C) a society's wants and needs are limited
    (D) a society's wants and needs can all be satisfied
    (E) material resources are not limited

50. A production possibilities curve is based on which assumption?
    (A) Resources are unlimited.
    (B) Technology is not used to its full potential.
    (C) A nation's economy only produces two different goods.
    (D) A nation's economy can produce hundreds of different goods.
    (E) Some unemployment is present.

51. What would cause the production possibilities curve to shift to the left?
    (A) government investment in public education
    (B) a hurricane that damaged several major cities
    (C) an increase in the birth rate
    (D) an increase in immigration
    (E) government investment in highways, airports, and other infrastructure

52. If two nations begin trading goods with one another
    (A) consumption will increase for both nations
    (B) only the nation with an absolute advantage will benefit from trade
    (C) consumption will decrease for both nations
    (D) consumption will not change in either nation
    (E) production possibilities curves for both countries will shift to the right

53. A nation produces sugar and cars. If the nations production possibilities curve bows outward, increasing the production of sugar will cause car production to do which of the following?
    (A) fall at a decreasing rate
    (B) fall at a constant rate
    (C) fall at an increasing rate
    (D) rise at a decreasing rate
    (E) rise at an increasing rate

54. A nation produces bread and cake. If the nation's production possibilities curve is represented as linear (a downward-sloping straight line), increasing the production of bread will cause cake production to do which of the following?
    (A) fall at a decreasing rate
    (B) fall at a constant rate
    (C) fall at an increasing rate
    (D) rise at a decreasing rate
    (E) rise at a constant rate

55. Quantity demanded and the price of a good have an inverse relationship. This is known as
    (A) the law of supply
    (B) the law of demand
    (C) the law of increasing opportunity costs
    (D) ceteris paribus
    (E) central planning

56. Efficient prices within a market economy are determined by which of the following?
    (A) the interaction of supply and demand for that good or service
    (B) the producers of that good or service
    (C) the consumers of that good or service
    (D) the government controlling that good or service
    (E) the quantity of the good or service

57. Quantity supplied will be equal to quantity demanded if which of the following occurs?

(A) An effective price ceiling is present.
(B) An effective price floor is present.
(C) Goods are exchanged in a market economy.
(D) Goods are exchanged in a command economy.
(E) A central planning board makes output decisions.

	Computers in a day	Bicycles in a day
Steve	50	100
Todd	30	90

58. Using the preceding data, consider this question: Does Steve have an absolute or a comparative advantage in either the production of computers and bicycles?

	Computers	**Bicycles**
(A)	absolute only	absolute and comparative
(B)	comparative only	comparative only
(C)	absolute and comparative	absolute only
(D)	comparative only	absolute and comparative
(E)	absolute only	absolute only

59. The main difference between a shortage and scarcity is

(A) there is no difference between the two terms
(B) only resources are scarce, but a shortage can be corrected by increasing production
(C) all things are scarce, but a shortage represents excess demand for a good or service
(D) only goods and services can be scarce
(E) scarcity is represented by excess supply of goods and services, but a shortage is represented by excess demand for goods and services

60. If a country has an absolute advantage over another country

(A) it can produce more of one good than the other country can
(B) it gives up less of one good to produce the other good
(C) it gives up more of one good to produce the other good
(D) it should not engage in international trade with the other country
(E) it can produce less of one good than the other country can

61. A market for a good or service is represented by which of the following?

    (A) a production possibilities frontier
    (B) the price of that good or service
    (C) the consumers for that good or service
    (D) the interaction of supply and demand
    (E) the quantity of the good or service

62. The determinants of demand do NOT include

    (A) consumer tastes and preferences
    (B) income levels
    (C) price levels for substitute goods
    (D) consumer price expectations
    (E) production capacity

63. The determinants of supply do NOT include

    (A) price levels for production inputs
    (B) consumer tastes
    (C) the number of suppliers in the market
    (D) tax rates
    (E) technology

64. An increase in consumer incomes allows consumers to purchase larger quantities of all goods. What is this known as?

    (A) income effect
    (B) substitution effect
    (C) law of increasing cost
    (D) law of demand
    (E) law of supply

Use the following graph for questions 65–67.

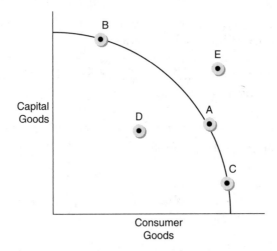

65. This economy has decided to concentrate their efforts to move their economy toward growth. The movement that would allow for the most opportunity for growth would be?

(A) moving production from Point A to Point E
(B) moving production from Point A to Point D
(C) moving production from Point C to Point B
(D) moving production from Point B to Point C
(E) moving production from Point A to Point B

66. According to this production possibilities curve, the best place to produce would be at which point?

(A) Point A, B, or C
(B) Point C only
(C) Point E only
(D) Point D only
(E) Point B only

67. Now assume that this economy is moving out of a recession. The movement that would best represent a recovering economy would be

(A) moving production from Point A to Point E
(B) moving production from Point D to Point A
(C) moving production from Point C to Point B
(D) moving production from Point B to Point C
(E) moving production from Point A to Point B

Use the following graph for questions 68–70.

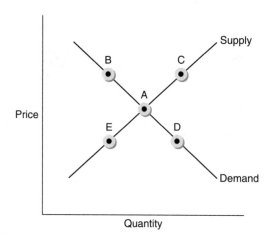

68. This market is at equilibrium at which point?
    (A) Point D
    (B) Point A
    (C) Point B
    (D) Point C
    (E) Point E

69. A shortage is represented in this market between which two points?
    (A) Point D and Point E
    (B) Point A and Point C
    (C) Point B and Point C
    (D) Point C and Point E
    (E) Point B and Point D

70. A surplus is represented in this market between which two points?
    (A) Point D and Point E
    (B) Point A and Point C
    (C) Point B and Point C
    (D) Point C and Point E
    (E) Point B and Point D

CHAPTER 2

Economic Indicators and the Business Cycle

71. The circular flow model illustrates
    (A) that workers, entrepreneurs, and owners of land and capital offer their services through product markets
    (B) the structures of both command and capitalist economic systems
    (C) that workers, entrepreneurs, and owners of land and capital offer their services through national agencies
    (D) how the Federal Reserve buys and sells bonds to stimulate the economy
    (E) that workers, entrepreneurs, and owners of land and capital offer their services through a resource market

72. In the simple circular flow model
    (A) individuals and householders are sellers of resources and demanders of products
    (B) householders are sellers of products and demanders of resources
    (C) the GDP is represented by the number of households and businesses in the economy
    (D) businesses are sellers of resources and demanders of products
    (E) businesses are sellers of products and sellers of resources

73. If you wanted to understand the relationship between households, businesses, and resources, you would study
    (A) the circular flow model
    (B) the equilibrium point of supply and demand
    (C) nonmarket transactions
    (D) aggregate supply
    (E) aggregate demand

74. When economists refer to the gross domestic product (GDP), they mean

(A) all final goods and services produced in an economy in a year

(B) all intermediate and final goods and services produced in an economy in a year

(C) all final goods and services produced in an economy in a five-year time period

(D) all final goods and services produced in an economy in a year, including overseas branches and divisions

(E) the total expenditure of consumer and government spending in an economy in a given year

75. Gross domestic product does NOT include

(A) government spending

(B) consumer income

(C) net income from foreign investments

(D) consumer spending minus government investments

(E) A and C

76. Which of the following is a limitation of the use of GDP as an indicator of economic performance?

(A) It does not include investment by corporations.

(B) It does not include changes in consumer habits.

(C) It does not include taxes.

(D) It does not include imports.

(E) It does not include time spent volunteering.

77. Which of the following are considered leakages from the circular flow model?

(A) taxes and savings

(B) taxes and the price of capital goods

(C) savings and the price of natural resources

(D) taxes and interest rates

(E) interest rates and automatic stabilizers

78. An example of a final good calculated into the GDP for the year
    would be
    (A) a computer chip bought by IBM to be used in a computer
    (B) a used car sold to a consumer
    (C) a new car sold to a consumer
    (D) the lumber used to construct a new house
    (E) all of the above

79. In the circular flow model, the factors of production
    (A) are owned by businesses
    (B) are owned by households
    (C) are owned by a central government
    (D) are only obtained through international trade
    (E) are owned by central banks

    not final goods

80. An intermediate good is not included in the calculation of GDP
    because
    (A) it would double count those items
    (B) they are not sold in a market transaction
    (C) it does not include taxes
    (D) it does not include imports
    (E) it does not include time spent volunteering

81. All of the following would be included in the expenditure approach
    to calculate GDP EXCEPT
    (A) consumer spending
    (B) government investments $C + I + G + X_n$
    (C) private investments
    (D) savings
    (E) net exports

82. The fact that the government is included in the circular flow model
    shows that the government
    (A) provides goods and services to businesses and households
    (B) maintains a strong control on economic resources and sells a
        portion of them on the open market
    (C) obtains revenues in the open market
    (D) does not provide goods and services to businesses and
        households
    (E) A, B, and C only

83. The formula for calculating gross domestic product is

(A) C + I + G – (X + M)
(B) C – I + G + (X – M)
(C) C + G + (X – M)
(D) (C + G)(I + (X – M))
(E) C + I + G + (X – M)

84. Jason and Mary purchased a new house in 2012 for $300,000. This purchase would be included in the GDP as

(A) consumer savings
(B) government investment
(C) investment
(D) consumption of private fixed capital
(E) consumer spending

85. Investments in the U.S. economy rise from $150 billion to $250 billion. The initial increase in GDP would be equal to

(A) a decrease GDP by $100 billion
(B) an increase GDP by $100 billion
(C) a decrease GDP by $250 billion
(D) an increase GDP by $50 billion
(E) There would be no change in GDP for that year.

Use the following data to answer question 86. The information is in billions of dollars.

Personal consumption:	$1,000
Personal taxes:	$10
U.S. exports:	$150
U.S. imports:	$175
Contributions to Social Security:	$200
Private domestic investments:	$350
Government investments:	$600
Corporate income tax:	$35

86. Based on the information in the preceding chart, the GDP would be calculated as

   (A) $1,925 billion
   (B) $2,150 billion
   (C) $2,500 billion
   (D) $1,675 billion
   (E) $1,950 billion

87. The most significant difference between nominal GDP and real GDP is

   (A) the value of current production at the current prices
   (B) expressing the changing value of prices over time
   (C) using prices from a fixed point in time
   (D) utilizing the consumer price index
   (E) calculating fluctuations in stock market prices

88. If the nominal GDP for 2011 was $200 billion and the price index was 90, real GDP would be

   (A) more than $200 billion
   (B) less than $200 billion
   (C) equal to $200 billion
   (D) equal to gross imports minus gross exports
   (E) none of the above

89. Joe recently graduated from college with a degree in history. He is discouraged that he will not find a job due to tough economic times. He decides not to actively pursue a job but to wait for the economy to turn for the better. Joe is considered

   (A) structurally unemployed
   (B) frictionally unemployed
   (C) cyclically unemployed
   (D) seasonally unemployed
   (E) not part of the labor force

90. The labor force is defined as

(A) individuals who are working or looking for a job
(B) the percentage of people who are not working
(C) individuals who are working, looking for a job, or not working and not looking for a job
(D) all individuals who are working or looking for work divided by the number of people cyclically unemployed
(E) individuals who work at least 15 hours per week

91. Elaine quit her job as a teaching assistant and went back to school to be a guidance counselor. Last year she received her master's degree and is currently looking for a job. Elaine is considered

(A) cyclically unemployed
(B) frictionally unemployed — reuit prere, scube inng
(C) structurally unemployed — technology/skills
(D) seasonally unemployed
(E) not part of the labor force

92. Full employment occurs when

(A) cyclical unemployment does not exist
(B) seasonal unemployment does not exist
(C) frictional unemployment does not exist
(D) structural unemployment does not exist
(E) both cyclical and frictional unemployment do not exist

93. Two good measures of inflation are the

(A) consumer price index and the natural rate of unemployment
(B) consumer price index and the producer price index
(C) producer price index and the natural rate of unemployment
(D) consumer price index and the rate of stagflation
(E) producer price index and the rate of stagflation

94. Stagflation occurs when

(A) real GDP increases and price levels decrease
(B) real GDP decreases and price levels decrease
(C) unemployment and price levels increase
(D) nominal GDP decreases and price levels increase
(E) GDP decreases and the price level decreases

95. If a teacher loses his or her job because students' parents move out of the area due to a poor economy, he or she would be considered
(A) cyclically unemployed — too far phelos
(B) seasonally unemployed
(C) frictionally unemployed
(D) structurally unemployed
(E) not part of the labor force

Refer to the following chart to answer questions 96 and 97.

Employed:	8,000
Unemployed:	1,000
Not in the labor force:	500

96. According to the chart, what is the unemployment rate?
(A) 10%
(B) 15%
(C) 11%
(D) 5%
(E) 7%

97. According to the chart, what is the size of the labor force?
(A) 7,500
(B) 9,000
(C) 9,500
(D) 6,500
(E) The size is unknowable because the number of cyclically unemployed workers is not given.

98. Cycling Cyclist Inc. had an inventory of 100 bicycles last year. Its current inventory is 120 bicycles. Last year it sold 90 bikes for $50 per bicycle. What is the value of output that would be included in the GDP for last year?
(A) $5,500
(B) $3,500
(C) $1,000
(D) $5,000
(E) $4,500

$80 + (120 - 100) =$

$80 + 20 = 110 \cdot 50\$$

99. If the president of the United States wanted to measure inflation from 2003 to 2010, he or she would most likely examine the

(A) gross national product
(B) consumer price index
(C) Federal Reserve Bank
(D) gross domestic product
(E) all of the above

100. Which of the following would not be harmed by unexpected inflation?

(A) a business that has a long-term contract providing service for another business
(B) a cost-of-living adjustment granted to a teachers' union
(C) banks that loan money at a fixed rate of interest
(D) money in an account earning less than the actual rate of inflation
(E) individuals that have a fixed income

101. The value of output produced in England by a U.S. fast food restaurant would be

(A) included in the United States GDP
(B) included in both United States and England's GDP
(C) included in England's GDP
(D) not included in England's GDP
(E) not included in either the United States or England's GDP

102. Jessica received her college degree in computer science and was offered a job at IBM. She decides to take a year off and travel throughout Europe. What effect would this decision have on the unemployment rate?

(A) an increase in the unemployment rate
(B) a decrease in the unemployment rate
(C) an increase in cyclical unemployment
(D) a decrease in structural unemployment
(E) no change in the unemployment rate

103. A person who is neither working nor looking for work is considered to be

(A) frictionally unemployed
(B) unemployed
(C) structurally unemployed
(D) part of the labor force
(E) outside of the labor force

104. Hyperinflation refers to

(A) a rapid increase in the price level
(B) a gradual increase in the price level
(C) a rapid increase in the price level, but money remains a good store of value
(D) a decline in real GDP
(E) a decrease in nominal GDP

105. Suppose the gross domestic product is $15 million, where consumer spending is $4 million, investments are $2 million, government spending is $5 million, and exports are $4 million. How much is spent on imports?

(A) $2 million
(B) $3 million
(C) $5 million
(D) $4 million
(E) $0

$15 = 4 + 2 + 5 + 4$

M

106. All of the following would be calculated into the GDP EXCEPT

(A) the sale of marshmallows to an ice-cream producer
(B) the sale of a new car
(C) the sale of a new truck exported from America
(D) government-purchased weapons for the military
(E) a person paying rent for an apartment

107. When constructing a price index, a base year refers to

(A) the average price level of goods and services
(B) a point of reference to compare real values over time
(C) the percentage change in the price index over time
(D) the top of the business cycle signaling the end of expansion
(E) a collection of goods and services that represent what is consumed in an economy for the year

108. All of the following are examples of an underground economy EXCEPT

(A) selling illegal drugs
(B) paying cash to a babysitter
(C) bartering
(D) buying a used car from a car dealership
(E) taking cash for a second job and not reporting the income to the IRS

109. Nominal GDP refers to

(A) the value of current production, but using prices from a set point in time
(B) the value of current production, but using prices gathered over the past five years
(C) the value of current production at current prices
(D) prices at the peak of the business cycle
(E) the value of current production at the trough of the business cycle subtracted from that at the peak of the business cycle

110. In the circular flow model, the factors of production are traded

(A) in the stock market
(B) in the resource market
(C) in the product market
(D) in the foreign exchange market
(E) by the central government

111. The government interacts with all of the following parts of the circular flow EXCEPT

(A) product market
(B) factor market
(C) firms
(D) exports
(E) households

112. A final good included in GDP would include

(A) steel purchased by an automaker
(B) flour purchased by a breadmaker
(C) concrete purchased by a construction company
(D) a television set purchased by a consumer
(E) sheets of wood purchased by a cabinet maker

113. A good that would NOT be included in GDP would be

(A) a new truck
(B) a box of soft drinks
(C) a used truck
(D) a loaf of bread
(E) a hamburger

114. GDP does NOT include

(A) net exports
(B) income earned abroad
(C) government spending
(D) private investments
(E) net imports

115. In the circular flow model,

(A) businesses purchase resources
(B) businesses purchase goods
(C) consumers purchase resources
(D) the Federal Reserve purchases resources
(E) goods are obtained primarily through international trade

116. Suppose government spending increased from $800 billion to $900 billion for the year while other components of the GDP did not change. The GDP would

(A) rise by $100 billion
(B) fall by $100 billion
(C) rise by $50 billion
(D) fall by $200 billion
(E) remain unchanged

117. Gross domestic product includes

(A) used goods
(B) intermediate goods
(C) net imports
(D) goods produced abroad
(E) savings

118. What is the correct sequence of events that is shown by the traditional business cycle?

(A) peak, trough, contraction, expansion, recovery
(B) trough, contraction, peak, expansion, recovery
(C) recovery, trough, expansion, contraction, peak
(D) contraction, peak, trough, contraction, recovery
(E) expansion, peak, contraction, trough, recovery

119. Which of the following are considered injections into the circular flow model?

(A) government spending and consumer spending
(B) government spending and investment
(C) investment and savings
(D) interest rates and investment
(E) savings and government spending

120. In the circular flow model, a leakage would flow into

(A) imports
(B) firms
(C) households
(D) product markets
(E) factor markets

Use the following data to answer question 121. The information is in billions of dollars.

U.S. exports	$100
U.S. imports	$200
Personal consumption	$2,000
Private domestic investments	$500
Corporate income tax	$50
Government investments	$1,000

121. What is GDP?

(A) $3,500
(B) $3,400
(C) $3,450
(D) $3,550
(E) $3,600

122. If the price index falls from 150 to 75,

(A) consumer purchasing power increases by 100 percent
(B) the price of every good is reduced by 50 percent
(C) consumer purchasing power decreases by 50 percent
(D) the price of every good increases by 100 percent
(E) consumer income increases

123. If the price index increases from 70 to 210,

(A) consumer purchasing power increases by 300 percent
(B) the price of every good increases by 300 percent
(C) the price of a select basket of goods increases by 300 percent
(D) consumer purchasing power increases by 67 percent
(E) consumer income decreases

124. If the nominal GDP for 2016 was $400 billion and the price index was 120, real GDP would be

(A) less than $400 billion
(B) equal to $400 billion
(C) more than $400 billion
(D) equal to government investment minus taxes
(E) equal to net exports

if more than 100.
its less

125. Bob graduated from college with a degree in biology, but employers decide not to hire Bob because they are looking for college graduates with computer science degrees. Bob is considered

(A) structurally unemployed
(B) frictionally unemployed
(C) cyclically unemployed
(D) seasonally unemployed
(E) not part of the labor force

126. A government can best reduce structural unemployment by

(A) offering job training programs
(B) lowering tax rates
(C) increasing imports
(D) increasing government spending
(E) expanding the money supply

127. Workers who are employed part-time are considered

(A) unemployed
(B) employed
(C) not in the labor force
(D) cyclically unemployed
(E) structurally unemployed

128. Bob decided he no longer wants to work as a chef. He quit his chef job and is currently looking for a job as a truck driver. Bob is considered

(A) cyclically unemployed
(B) frictionally unemployed
(C) structurally unemployed
(D) seasonally unemployed
(E) not part of the labor force

129. If a country has a total population of 200 million, there are 10 million unemployed workers, and 20 million people are not looking for work, the size of the labor force is

(A) 200 million
(B) 190 million
(C) 170 million
(D) 180 million
(E) 210 million

130. If a country has a total population of 300 million, there are 250 million employed people in the workforce, and 20 million people are not looking for work, the number of unemployed workers is

(A) 50 million
(B) 40 million
(C) 30 million
(D) 20 million
(E) 70 million

131. A country has a total population of 100 million people. If 10 million people are not in the labor force and 20 million people are unemployed, the number of employed workers is
    (A) 80 million
    (B) 70 million
    (C) 110 million
    (D) 90 million
    (E) 130 million

132. United Television had an inventory of 200 television sets last year. Its current inventory is 150 television sets. Last year it sold 100 television sets for $100 per set. What output would be included in the GDP for last year?
    (A) $10,000
    (B) $15,000
    (C) $5,000
    (D) $20,000
    (E) $25,000

133. Federated Automobiles had an inventory of 50 cars last year. Its current inventory is 80 cars. Last year it sold 60 cars for $10,000 each. What output would be included in the GDP for last year?
    (A) $500,000
    (B) $600,000
    (C) $800,000
    (D) $900,000
    (E) $1,200,000

134. If the inflation rate is –2 percent, this is known as
    (A) disinflation
    (B) deflation
    (C) inflation
    (D) biflation
    (E) depreciation

135. If the inflation rate decreases from 2 percent to 1.5 percent, this is known as

(A) disinflation
(B) deflation
(C) inflation
(D) biflation
(E) depreciation

136. If consumption is equal to $100, government spending is equal to $250, exports are equal to $50, investment is equal to $75, imports are equal to $75, and taxes are equal to $25, GDP would be equal to

(A) $575
(B) $550
(C) $400
(D) $450
(E) $525

$100 + 250 + 50 + 75$
75

137. If a factory closes down because a recession has reduced demand for its products, the workers who lost their jobs at the factory are

(A) cyclically unemployed
(B) seasonally unemployed
(C) frictionally unemployed
(D) structurally unemployed
(E) not part of the labor force

138. Students who are taking courses at a university and are not searching for work, even though local businesses are hiring, are considered

(A) cyclically unemployed
(B) seasonally unemployed
(C) frictionally unemployed
(D) structurally unemployed
(E) not part of the labor force

139. Midwest Appliances had an inventory of 250 refrigerators last year. Its current inventory is 200 refrigerators. Last year it sold 300 refrigerators for $400 each. What output would be included in the GDP for last year?

(A) $120,000
(B) $140,000
(C) $80,000
(D) $100,000
(E) $160,000

350×400

140. East Coast Ovens had an inventory of 400 ovens last year. Its current inventory is 500 ovens. Last year it sold 250 ovens for $100 each. What output would be included in the GDP for last year?

(A) $35,000
(B) $25,000
(C) $40,000
(D) $30,000
(E) $50,000

141. Sally decides to purchase an apartment complex. She would like to earn a 10 percent return on the apartment complex. If the current rate of inflation is –2 percent, what return does Sally need to invest in the apartment complex?

(A) 12 percent
(B) 10 percent
(C) 8 percent
(D) 14 percent
(E) 6 percent

142. Joe decides to quit his job at an auto repair shop and go on a hiking trip for several months. How would this decision affect the unemployment rate?

(A) an increase in the unemployment rate
(B) a decrease in the unemployment rate
(C) an increase in cyclical unemployment
(D) a decrease in structural unemployment
(E) no change in the unemployment rate

143. Deflation refers to

(A) an increase in the price level
(B) a rapid increase in the price level
(C) an increase in the prices of some goods, while the prices of other goods decrease
(D) a decrease in the price level
(E) a decrease in real GDP

144. Using the following information, calculate the real rate of interest. Current rate of inflation is equal to 3%, current rate of interest is equal to 5%, and taxes are equal to 2%.

(A) 6%
(B) 10%
(C) 8%
(D) 2%
(E) 5%

145. A recent college graduate searching for a job would classified as what form of unemployment?

(A) structurally unemployed
(B) employed
(C) not in the labor force
(D) cyclically unemployed
(E) frictionally unemployed

146. If the gross domestic product is $20 million, investments are $5 million, government spending is $4 million, exports are $3 million, and imports are $6 million, what is consumer spending?

(A) $10 million
(B) $11 million
(C) $14 million
(D) $17 million
(E) $24 million

147. If the gross domestic product is 25 million, investments are $8 million, government spending is $6 million, consumer spending is $10 million, and exports are $5 million, what are imports?

(A) $4 million
(B) $6 million
(C) $5 million
(D) $8 million
(E) $2 million

148. GDP calculations would NOT include

(A) the sale of a new airplane to an airline
(B) government construction expenses for a superhighway
(C) grocery receipts from a supermarket
(D) the sale of sheet metal to an auto factory
(E) rent paid by a law firm for its office space

149. Transactions in the underground economy would include

(A) the purchase of auto insurance from an insurance company
(B) the purchase of groceries using a credit card
(C) a cash loan from a credit union
(D) an exchange of two used cars that was not reported to tax authorities
(E) a cash withdrawal from an ATM

150. The value of a price index is

(A) base index value divided by current value
(B) current value divided by base index value
(C) base index value plus current value
(D) base index value minus current value
(E) base index value multiplied by current value

151. The consumer price index overstates the true rate of inflation because

(A) consumers' substitution bias is not considered
(B) producers' increase in labor costs are not considered
(C) consumers do not frequently change their spending habits
(D) it does not include renting of apartments
(E) the market basket never changes

152. If the current price of a basket of goods is $300 and the price in the base year was $200, when the index was 100, the price index will be

(A) 200
(B) 150
(C) 50
(D) 300
(E) 100

price increased by 50%

$\frac{200-100\%}{300} -x$

100+50

153. If the current price of a basket of goods is 20 percent less than the price in the base year, when the index was 100, the price index will be

(A) 120
(B) 20
(C) 80
(D) 90
(E) 200

154. If a country has a total population of 500 million, there are 400 million employed people in the workforce, and 40 million people are not looking for work, the number of unemployed workers is

(A) 100 million
(B) 60 million
(C) 40 million
(D) 80 million
(E) 200 million

155. A country has a total population of 240 million people. If 30 million people are not in the labor force and 20 million people are unemployed, the number of employed workers is

(A) 200 million
(B) 210 million
(C) 190 million
(D) 170 million
(E) 150 million

156. If a crab fishing boat hires fishing workers for a few months but lays them off once the crab catch is brought in for the year, the fishing workers are considered

(A) cyclically unemployed
(B) seasonally unemployed
(C) frictionally unemployed
(D) structurally unemployed
(E) not part of the labor force

157. If the gross domestic product is 30 million, investments are $10 million, government spending is $7 million, consumer spending is $15 million, and imports are $11 million, what are exports?

(A) $7 million
(B) $9 million
(C) $11 million
(D) $13 million
(E) $15 million

158. If the price index for 1990 is 100, a basket of selected goods costs $200 in 1990, and a basket of selected goods costs $240 in 1995, the price index for 1995 is

(A) 100
(B) 110
(C) 120
(D) 130
(E) 140

159. The GDP calculation would include

  I. Corn meal purchased by a corn dog manufacturer
  II. Sugar purchased by a cookie manufacturer
  III. Cupcake frosting purchased by a consumer

(A) I only
(B) II only
(C) III only
(D) I and II
(E) II and III

160. If the price index falls from 160 to 120,

(A) the price of every good increases by 50 percent
(B) the price of every good increases by 100 percent
(C) consumer purchasing power increases by 50 percent
(D) consumer purchasing power decreases by 50 percent
(E) consumer income decreases

161. If the price index increases from 60 to 90,

(A) the price of every good increases by 50 percent
(B) consumer income increases
(C) consumer purchasing power decreases by 50 percent
(D) the price of a select basket of goods increases by 50 percent
(E) wages decrease

162. If a country has a total population of 150 million, there are 20 million unemployed workers, and 5 million people are not looking for work, the size of the labor force is

(A) 150 million
(B) 145 million
(C) 140 million
(D) 135 million
(E) 130 million

163. If a country has a population of 180 million, there are 120 million employed people in the country, and 10 million people are not looking for work, the number of unemployed workers is

    (A) 60 million
    (B) 50 million
    (C) 40 million
    (D) 20 million
    (E) 10 million

164. Rocky Mountain Sports had an inventory of 500 tents last year. Its current inventory is 400 tents. Last year it sold 300 tents for $50 per tent. What output would be included in the GDP for last year?

    (A) $8,000
    (B) $10,000
    (C) $12,000
    (D) $14,000
    (E) $16,000

165. Which of the following would be helped by an unexpected increase in the rate of inflation?

    (A) borrowers who take loans at an adjustable rate
    (B) lenders who lend at a fixed rate
    (C) borrowers who take out loans at a fixed rate
    (D) consumers on a fixed income
    (E) workers who do not have a cost of living clause in their contract

166. Which of the following would not be included in the calculation of United States GDP?

    (A) a new Japanese car manufactured in Kentucky
    (B) sugar purchased by a cookie manufacturer
    (C) cupcake frosting purchased by your mother
    (D) an aircraft carrier purchased by the government
    (E) the building of a new home

167. Bob works at an auto factory. He does a good job and receives a 5 percent wage increase at the end of the year. The inflation rate for that year was 3 percent. How much has Bob's real income increased?
    (A) 2%
    (B) 3%
    (C) 4%
    (D) 5%
    (E) 8%

168. Mark works at a fast-food restaurant and earns minimum wage. The state raised the minimum wage from $10 per hour to $12 per hour at the end of the year. Inflation for the year was 5 percent. By what percentage has Mark's real income increased?
    (A) 10 percent
    (B) 15 percent
    (C) 20 percent
    (D) 25 percent
    (E) 50 percent

169. Disinflation is defined as
    (A) a decrease in the rate of inflation below zero
    (B) the increasing rate of inflation combined with an equal increase in unemployment
    (C) an increase of the general price level
    (D) a decrease of the general price level
    (E) the government and Federal Reserve engaging in policies to actively decrease the rate of inflation

170. The most accurate definition for stagflation is
    (A) when the economy experiences high rates of inflation and unemployment simultaneously
    (B) when the economy is experiencing a depression
    (C) when the economy is experiencing a high rate of inflation
    (D) when unemployment and inflation move in opposite directions
    (E) when unemployment decreases rapidly

CHAPTER 3

National Income and Price Determination

171. The aggregate demand curve slopes downward because

(A) a higher price level makes production costs increase

(B) quantity demanded decreases as price increases

(C) the amount of expenditures to each production unit illustrates the amount of output

(D) production costs decline as real output increases

(E) both A and B

172. When cyclical unemployment is zero, and structural unemployment is very low, this is considered

(A) full employment

(B) the equilibrium price at full employment

(C) the velocity of money

(D) the quantity theory of money

(E) cost-push inflation

173. The multiplier effect refers to

(A) government regulations that affect the GDP

(B) any change in aggregate expenditures always decreases GDP

(C) any change in aggregate expenditures creates a bigger change in GDP

(D) the MPS will always be greater than 1

(E) none of the above

174. All of the following will cause the aggregate demand curve to shift EXCEPT

(A) a change in consumer income

(B) a change in price level

(C) a decrease in government spending

(D) an increase in net exports

(E) an increase in net imports

175. Which of the following factors will shift the aggregate supply curve to the right?

(A) an increase in productivity

(B) increased wages for workers

(C) an increase in government regulations

(D) consumer income increases

(E) none of the above

176. The aggregate supply curve

(A) is best explained by the interest rate effect

(B) shows the amount of real output that producers are willing and able to produce at each price level

(C) is upward sloping because of the real balances effect

(D) reflects the amount of real output that consumers are willing and able to purchase at each price level

(E) becomes vertical in the short run

177. Other things being equal, a shift of the aggregate supply curve to the left could be caused by all of the following EXCEPT

(A) an increase in government regulation

(B) a decrease in workers' wages

(C) a decrease in the labor force

(D) an increase in taxes

(E) a decrease in productivity

178. The interest rate effect suggests

(A) a decrease in the money supply will increase interest rates
(B) an increase in the price level will increase the demand for money
(C) an increase in the price level will lead consumers and businesses to borrow more money, which increases the interest rate
(D) a decrease in the price level will lead consumers and businesses to borrow more money, which increases the interest rate
(E) an increase in the price level will lead consumers and businesses to borrow less money, which increases the interest rate

179. The multiplier effect will be greater on aggregate demand if

(A) there is no increase in the price level
(B) both aggregate demand and aggregate supply increase
(C) both aggregate demand and aggregate supply decrease
(D) aggregate demand increases and aggregate supply decreases
(E) cannot be determined because the up-to-date foreign exchange rate is not given

180. Imagine that investment increases by $10 billion and the MPC (marginal propensity to consume) is 0.8. In the long run, the aggregate demand curve will shift

(A) leftward by $30 billion at each price level
(B) rightward by $5 billion at each price level
(C) rightward by $80 billion at each price level
(D) leftward by $18 billion at each price level
(E) rightward by $50 billion at each price level

181. Inflation will most likely occur when

(A) aggregate supply and aggregate demand increase
(B) aggregate supply and aggregate demand decrease
(C) aggregate supply decreases and aggregate demand increases
(D) aggregate supply increases and aggregate demand decreases
(E) a price ceiling is placed above the equilibrium point between aggregate supply and aggregate demand

182. The government increases the minimum wage. How will this increase in labor costs affect the economy in the short run?

    (A) Short-run aggregate supply will decrease.
    (B) Aggregate demand will increase.
    (C) Long-run aggregate supply will increase.
    (D) Aggregate demand will decrease.
    (E) Short-run aggregate supply will increase.

183. Which of the following describes the aggregate supply curve in the long run?

    (A) It is horizontal.
    (B) It is always vertical.
    (C) It is upward sloping.
    (D) It is downward sloping.
    (E) It is horizontal at first, then becomes upward sloping.

184. Stagflation occurs when

    (A) aggregate demand increases and aggregate supply remains the same
    (B) aggregate demand remains the same and aggregate supply increases
    (C) there is a negative shock to aggregate supply
    (D) aggregate demand and aggregate supply increase
    (E) none of the above

185. Macroeconomic equilibrium occurs when

    (A) full-employment GDP exceeds equilibrium GDP
    (B) equilibrium GDP exceeds full-employment GDP
    (C) the quantity of real output demanded is equal to the quantity of real output supplied
    (D) there is a sustained falling price level
    (E) GDP falls for a consecutive six months

186. All of the following will decrease real GDP EXCEPT

    (A) an increase in government spending
    (B) an increase in the interest rate
    (C) a decrease in consumer income
    (D) a decrease in net exports
    (E) an increase in net imports

187. When the full-employment level exceeds the level of aggregate expenditures, which of the following most likely develops?
    (A) an inflationary gap
    (B) a recessionary gap
    (C) hyperinflation
    (D) stagflation
    (E) recession

188. The biggest difference between the Phillips curve in the short run and the Phillips curve in the long run is
    (A) an indirect relationship between inflation and unemployment in the short run, and a constant relationship in the long run
    (B) a constant relationship between inflation and unemployment in the short run, and an indirect relationship in the long run
    (C) a constant relationship between inflation and unemployment both in the short run and in the long run
    (D) a direct relationship between inflation and unemployment in the short run, and a constant relationship in the long run
    (E) a constant relationship between inflation and unemployment in the long run, and a positive relationship in the short run

189. The Phillips curve examines the relationship between
    (A) aggregate demand and aggregate supply
    (B) fiscal policy and monetary policy
    (C) inflation and unemployment
    (D) inflation and cyclical unemployment
    (E) recessionary gaps and inflationary gaps

190. A change in spending may generate even larger or smaller changes in real GDP. This is known as the
    (A) crowding out effect
    (B) velocity of money
    (C) quantity theory of money
    (D) multiplier effect
    (E) marginal propensity to save

191. The crowding out effect refers to the relationship between

(A) government spending/borrowing and private investment/consumption

(B) full employment and inflation

(C) unemployment and inflation

(D) government spending/borrowing and net exports/imports

(E) none of the above

192. Which of the following will cause the aggregate demand curve to shift to the right?

(A) an increase in the price level

(B) an increase in interest rates

(C) an increase in government spending

(D) a decrease in government spending

(E) a decrease in personal consumption

193. Which of the following illustrates a positive supply shock?

(A) discovery of new supplies of a natural resource

(B) a decrease in a natural resource

(C) a decrease in the labor force over a three-year period

(D) a decrease in the price of labor

(E) all of the above

194. An increase in government spending will

(A) generate more of an increase in national income due to the multiplier effect

(B) generate less national income due to the multiplier effect

(C) generate less of an increase in national income due to the net export effect

(D) generate more of an increase in national income due to the net export effect

(E) generate more of an increase in national income due to the interest rate effect

195. The best explanation why the aggregate supply curve is vertical in the long run is

    (A) enough time has passed for input prices to adjust to market forces

    (B) price level and output become equal

    (C) price level and full employment become equal

    (D) output and full employment become equal

    (E) the price of goods and services changes

196. Gross domestic product is the best indicator of

    (A) national income

    (B) the strength of the consumer price index

    (C) the strength of the Federal Reserve Bank

    (D) the strength of the producer price index

    (E) all of the above

197. John is a supply-side economist. If the United States is experiencing stagflation, which of the following actions would he be most willing to support?

    (A) the federal government increasing investment and spending

    (B) an increase to the money supply

    (C) the federal government decreasing investment and spending

    (D) decreasing income tax rates for the wealthy

    (E) none of the above

198. If the United States experienced another depression on the scale of the Great Depression of the 1930s, the government should take which of the following actions?

    (A) decrease government spending

    (B) increase government spending

    (C) increase taxes and increase government spending

    (D) increase taxes

    (E) none of the above

199. In the short run, the aggregate supply curve is

    (A) flat

    (B) upward sloping

    (C) vertical

    (D) downward sloping

    (E) undefined

200. The shape of the aggregate supply curve in the long run is

(A) flat
(B) upward sloping
(C) vertical
(D) downward sloping
(E) horizontal

201. Marginal propensity to consume will be higher for consumers with

(A) high incomes
(B) great wealth
(C) pension income
(D) no young children
(E) full-time jobs

202. Consumers with higher MPC are more likely to shop at businesses that are

(A) locally owned
(B) multinational firms
(C) in distant locations
(D) in foreign countries
(E) publicly traded

203. A positive GDP multiplier effect does NOT occur when

(A) investment increases
(B) government spending increases
(C) exports increase
(D) imports increase
(E) taxes decrease

204. The lowest GDP multiplier effect will result from

(A) an increase in government spending
(B) an increase in investment
(C) a decrease in taxes
(D) an increase in exports
(E) an increase in pensions

205. The aggregate demand curve would shift to the right if

(A) consumer income decreased
(B) the interest rate increased
(C) consumption decreased
(D) exports decreased
(E) imports decreased

206. The aggregate supply curve would shift to the left if

(A) productivity increased
(B) worker wages increased
(C) government regulations decreased
(D) taxes decreased
(E) consumer income increased

207. Assume the economy is currently in a recession. If the government takes no action to correct the recession, how will this effect aggregate demand, short-run aggregate supply, and unemployment in the long run?

	Aggregate Demand	**Aggregate Supply**	**Unemployment**
(A)	increase	unchanged	increase
(B)	increase	unchanged	decrease
(C)	decrease	increase	unchanged
(D)	unchanged	increase	decrease
(E)	increase	decrease	decrease

208. When the price level increases,

(A) interest rates will fall
(B) interest rates will be unaffected
(C) interest rates will rise
(D) demand for cash will decrease
(E) demand for investments will increase

209. If the price level in foreign countries increases and the price level in the United States remains the same,

(A) imports will increase
(B) imports will decrease
(C) imports will be unaffected
(D) exports will decrease
(E) exports will be unaffected

210. Which of the following would cause a decrease in exports from the United States?

(A) an appreciation of foreign currencies
(B) deflation in the United States
(C) an economic boom in Mexico
(D) a depreciation of the U.S. currency
(E) increasing inflation in the United States

211. If the price level increases, the multiplier effect will be

(A) lower
(B) undefined
(C) the same
(D) nonexistent
(E) higher

212. When the price level is falling and continues to fall, this is known as

(A) stagflation
(B) a recession
(C) deflation
(D) inflation
(E) a supply shock

213. An inflationary gap occurs when

(A) full-employment GDP exceeds equilibrium GDP
(B) equilibrium GDP exceeds full-employment GDP
(C) aggregate demand exceeds aggregate supply
(D) aggregate supply exceeds aggregate demand
(E) full-employment GDP is equal to equilibrium GDP

214. Which of the following illustrates a contractionary fiscal policy?

(A) an increase in taxation and a decrease in government spending
(B) an increase in taxation and an increase in government spending
(C) a decrease in taxation and a decrease in government spending
(D) no change in taxation and an increase in government spending
(E) an increase in taxation and no change in government spending

215. Decreasing government spending while increasing the tax rate would be the best policy for combating

(A) a recession
(B) inflation
(C) structural unemployment
(D) an expansionary fiscal policy
(E) a decreasing average price level

216. Deflation will most likely occur when

(A) aggregate supply and aggregate demand increase
(B) aggregate supply and aggregate demand decrease
(C) aggregate supply decreases and aggregate demand increases
(D) aggregate supply increases and aggregate demand decreases
(E) a price ceiling is placed above the equilibrium point between aggregate supply and aggregate demand

217. Cost-push inflation occurs when

(A) the price of a luxury good rises
(B) the price of a necessity good rises, and substitutes are available
(C) the price of a necessity good rises, and substitutes are not available
(D) the price of an inferior good rises
(E) the price of a necessity good falls

218. A positive shock to aggregate supply will result in

(A) stagflation
(B) a lower price level
(C) a recession
(D) a higher price level
(E) lower output

219. When total output demanded equals total output supplied, the nation is experiencing

(A) economic expansion
(B) a recession
(C) macroeconomic equilibrium
(D) hyperinflation
(E) a recessionary gap

220. Assume the economy is currently in an inflationary period. If the government takes no action to correct the rising inflation, how will this affect aggregate demand, short-run aggregate supply, and unemployment in the long run?

Aggregate Demand	**Aggregate Supply**	**Unemployment**
(A) increase	unchanged	increase
(B) increase	unchanged	decrease
(C) decrease	increase	unchanged
(D) increase	increase	decrease
(E) unchanged	decrease	increase

Refer to the following graph for questions 221–223.

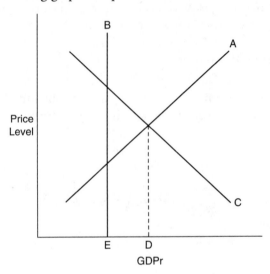

221. The negative relationship between the price level and real GDP is shown by which portion of the graph?
(A) A
(B) B
(C) C
(D) D
(E) E

222. The current state of the graph illustrates what macroeconomic concept?

(A) high unemployment
(B) a depressionary gap
(C) a recessionary gap
(D) an inflationary gap
(E) the long-run full employment level of real GDP

223. The full employment level of real GDP is located at what point on the graph?

(A) A
(B) B
(C) C
(D) D
(E) E

Refer to the following graph for questions 224 and 225.

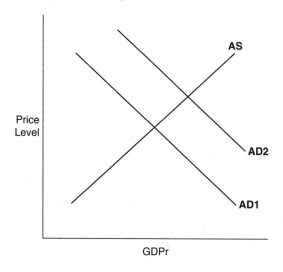

224. If aggregate demand moves from AD1 to AD2, it is likely that

(A) the economy is at full employment
(B) imports have risen
(C) government spending has decreased
(D) interest rates have risen
(E) consumption has increased

225. If aggregate demand shifts from AD2 to AD1, it is likely that inflation, unemployment, and GDP will change in which ways?

	Inflation	**GDP**	**Unemployment**
(A)	increase	unchanged	increase
(B)	increase	unchanged	decrease
(C)	decrease	decrease	increase
(D)	increase	increase	decrease
(E)	unchanged	decrease	increase

Refer to the following graph for questions 226 and 227.

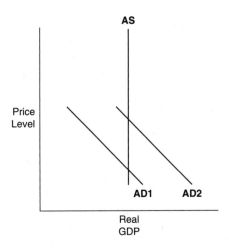

226. If aggregate demand moved from AD1 to AD2,

(A) output would increase
(B) employment would increase
(C) employment would decrease
(D) inflation would decrease
(E) inflation would increase

227. This graph shows an economy with

I. full employment
II. maximum output
III. underemployment

(A) I only
(B) II only
(C) I and II
(D) II and III
(E) III only

Refer to the following graph for questions 228 and 229.

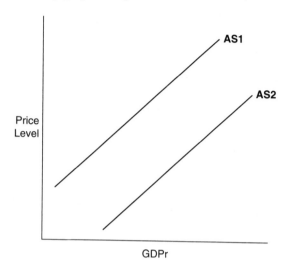

228. A shift in aggregate supply from AS1 to AS2 could be caused by
  (A) a lower unemployment rate
  (B) government infrastructure investments
  (C) an increase in raw material prices
  (D) an increase in transfer payments
  (E) an increase in the money supply

229. A shift in aggregate supply from AS1 to AS2 would NOT be caused by
  (A) an increase in immigration
  (B) the introduction of new technology
  (C) an increase in raw material prices
  (D) investment in human capital
  (E) a decrease in business taxes

230. When the level of aggregate expenditures exceeds the full-employment level, what is likely to occur?
  (A) an inflationary gap
  (B) a recessionary gap
  (C) deflation
  (D) macroeconomic equilibrium
  (E) recession

CHAPTER 4

The Financial Sector

231. Because any merchant will accept money in exchange for goods and services, money is useful as a

(A) unit of account
(B) medium of exchange
(C) store of value
(D) divisible system into M1, M2, and M3 money
(E) method to incur and pay back loans and debt

232. Which of the following would be considered a major component of the money supply M1?

(A) money market accounts
(B) checkable deposits
(C) bonds
(D) savings deposits
(E) all of the above

233. Anna recently celebrated her 18th birthday. In many of her birthday cards, she found slips of paper from the U.S. government promising to repay a loan at a fixed interest rate. These slips of paper are known as

(A) stocks
(B) bank loans
(C) shares
(D) bonds
(E) collateral

234. Which of the following is considered to be part of the M1 measurement of the money supply?
    (A) small time deposits
    (B) savings deposits
    (C) currency held by consumers
    (D) money market mutual funds
    (E) bonds

235. Which of the following is considered to be part of the M2 measurement of the money supply?
    (A) stocks
    (B) money in a 401(k)
    (C) currency held by consumers
    (D) mutual funds
    (E) bonds

236. Jacob transfers $2,000 from his savings account to his checking account. What effect will this transfer have on the M1 and M2 money supply?
    (A) M1 will increase and M2 will decrease.
    (B) M1 will increase and M2 will remain the same.
    (C) M1 will decrease and M2 will increase.
    (D) M1 will increase and M2 will increase.
    (E) The answer cannot be determined because the total checkable deposits in the economy are not given.

237. The United States backing of the money supply comes from
    (A) issuing Federal Reserve notes
    (B) using land and other natural resources as collateral
    (C) the full faith and credit of the U.S. government
    (D) backing by large quantities of precious metals such as gold and silver to cover the amount of paper money in circulation
    (E) all of the above

238. Both monetary and fiscal policy will have zero effect on real GDP
    (A) when the aggregate supply curve is in the long run
    (B) when the aggregate supply curve is in the short run
    (C) when contractionary policies are enacted by the Federal Reserve
    (D) when expansionary policies are enacted by the Federal Reserve
    (E) when expansionary policies are enacted by the Federal Reserve and contractionary fiscal policies are enacted by the U.S. government

239. The price of bonds and interest rates are

(A) positively related
(B) negatively related
(C) unrelated
(D) directly related
(E) cannot be determined because the CPI for the year is not given

240. The main function of the Federal Open Market Committee is

(A) buying and selling of securities to control the money supply and buying and selling government bonds
(B) monitoring the Federal Reserve banks
(C) monitoring the checkable deposits of commercial banks
(D) enforcing financial securities laws
(E) monitoring the fluctuations in the money supply

241. Consumers will NOT tend to purchase more goods and services using credit if

(A) interest rates are increased
(B) interest rates are decreased
(C) the marginal propensity to save (MPS) is decreased
(D) the marginal propensity to consume (MPC) is increased
(E) interest rates remain the same

242. The most important function of the Federal Reserve System is

(A) controlling the money supply
(B) issuing currency
(C) lending money to commercial banks
(D) overseeing the transactions between commercial banks and consumers
(E) informing the U.S. government of fluctuations in the money supply

243. Currency and checkable deposits held by the Federal Reserve and U.S. government

(A) are backed by its equal value of gold and silver
(B) help decrease the rate of inflation
(C) inadvertently increase the rate of inflation
(D) may only be counted as a store of value
(E) are not included in the M1 money supply

244. The money creation process within an economy is mainly controlled by whom?

(A) consumers
(B) Federal Reserve banks
(C) Congress
(D) banks
(E) the money market

245. If interest rates increase, there will be

(A) an increase in the demand for money
(B) a decrease in the total amount of money demanded
(C) an increase in the total amount of money demanded
(D) a decrease in the total amount of money supplied
(E) an increase in the frequency of loans given at commercial banks

246. The buying and selling of Treasury securities to stimulate or slow the economy is called

(A) open market operations
(B) fiscal policy
(C) investment
(D) government spending
(E) money creation

247. If the required reserve ratio is 25 percent and a commercial bank has $2 million in cash, $1 million in government securities, $3 million on deposit at a Federal Reserve bank, and $6 million in demand deposits, its total reserves are

(A) $3 million
(B) $4 million
(C) $5 million
(D) $8 million
(E) $12 million

248. If Leo deposits $150 in his checking account and later that day Leo's friend Terri negotiates a loan for $5,000 at the same bank, how will this affect the supply of money?

(A) increased by $5,000
(B) decreased by $5,000
(C) increased by $4,850
(D) decreased by $4,850
(E) no change in the money supply

249. The process of a bank saving a portion of its checkable deposits and lending the remainder is referred to as

(A) open market operations
(B) fractional reserve banking
(C) investing
(D) money market mutual funds
(E) issuing stocks

250. A valid reason for requiring commercial banks to have reserve requirements is to

(A) ensure the banks have money for loans
(B) ensure the banks have enough money for withdrawals
(C) provide a system in which the transactions of banks may be monitored and controlled
(D) provide a system in which banks are held accountable for their transactions
(E) all of the above

251. Varying the money supply in an economy is beneficial because

(A) it will help during fluctuations in the business cycle
(B) it will push consumers to use currency over checkable deposits
(C) it will decrease inflation
(D) it will increase inflation
(E) it will decrease unemployment

252. M1 money supply refers to

(A) time accounts
(B) currency and credit card accounts
(C) coins and paper money held by the public and checkable deposits
(D) savings deposits and money market deposit accounts
(E) all of the above

253. M2 money supply refers to

(A) M1 money, savings accounts, time deposits, and noninstitutional money market funds
(B) savings accounts only
(C) time deposits only
(D) M1 money subtracted from M3 money
(E) none of the above

254. A shift of the money supply to the left was most likely caused by

(A) the Federal Reserve selling government securities on the open market
(B) the Federal Reserve buying government securities on the open market
(C) the Federal Reserve decreasing the discount rate
(D) the Federal Reserve lowering the reserve ratio
(E) an increase in government spending

255. A shift of the money supply to the left was possibly an attempt to

(A) decrease output of productivity
(B) decrease the current account surplus
(C) decrease inflation
(D) increase the price level
(E) stimulate the economy out of a recession

256. Which of the following reflects the two components of the demand for money?

(A) stocks and bonds
(B) checkable deposits and savings accounts
(C) buying and selling of government securities
(D) transactions demand and asset demand
(E) all of the above

257. A stock is

(A) a claim of ownership in a business
(B) a certificate of indebtedness
(C) traded in a closed market system
(D) a guarantee of future prices to be traded on the stock market
(E) all of the above

258. A bond is

(A) used if a business wants to raise money by borrowing money to be repaid plus a specific rate of interest
(B) a claim of ownership in a business
(C) not traded on the stock market
(D) rarely used in a free market system
(E) all of the above

259. If there is an increase in the money supply, then it was caused by
   (A) a decrease in the money supply
   (B) the Federal Reserve Bank
   (C) the federal government
   (D) a contractionary fiscal policy
   (E) none of the above

260. If Jack deposits $500 and the reserve ratio is 10 percent, what will result in the long term?
   (A) $4,500 in money creation
   (B) $5,000 in money destruction
   (C) $500 in money creation
   (D) $550 in money destruction
   (E) $50 in money creation

Use the following scenario to answer questions 261 and 262: Jennifer and Christopher are out shopping at their local mall. They walk pass a storefront window and see a sign that states, "Electronic back scratchers $50!"

261. In this scenario, money is serving which purpose?
   (A) store of value
   (B) unit of account
   (C) medium of exchange
   (D) checkable deposit
   (E) none of the above

262. Christopher decides to buy an electronic back scratcher. He brings it up to the counter and hands the cashier the money to purchase the product. In this scenario, money is serving as
   (A) a store of value
   (B) a unit of account
   (C) a checkable deposit
   (D) M1 money
   (E) a medium of exchange

263. All of the following are ways the Federal Reserve can change the money supply EXCEPT

(A) buying government securities
(B) selling government securities
(C) changing current tax rates
(D) changing the reserve ratio
(E) changing the discount rate

264. All of the following are assets held by Bank XYZ EXCEPT

(A) money on reserve
(B) loans made to businesses
(C) demand deposits
(D) loans made out to citizens
(E) a home mortgage

265. When currency/money is being used to establish prices of goods and services in an economy, it is being used as

(A) barter money
(B) a unit of account
(C) a medium of exchange
(D) a store of value
(E) commodity money

266. The Federal Reserve System is

(A) responsible for establishing monetary and fiscal policy
(B) responsible for establishing fiscal policy only
(C) the central bank of the United States
(D) only allowed to set interest rates
(E) only allowed to buy government securities

267. Currency in your wallet, traveler's checks, and checkable deposits represent

(A) M1 money supply
(B) M2 money supply
(C) M3 money supply
(D) M1 and M2 money supply
(E) M1 and M3 money supply

268. If the Federal Reserve lowered the reserve ratio to 5 percent, what would be the money multiplier?

(A) 20

(B) 10

(C) 5

(D) 50

(E) 25

269. All of the following will increase the money supply EXCEPT

(A) the Federal Reserve buying government securities

(B) the Federal Reserve decreasing the reserve ratio

(C) the Federal Reserve increasing the reserve ratio

(D) a decrease in the discount rate

(E) a decrease in taxes

270. The value of a bond will decrease if

(A) interest rates increase

(B) interest rates decrease

(C) a person does not cash the bond when it matures

(D) the Federal Reserve decides to sell government securities

(E) the Federal Reserve decides to buy government securities

271. A bank's biggest liability is

(A) mortgages

(B) investments in a money market

(C) bonds

(D) stocks

(E) checkable deposits

272. The value of a bond will decrease if

(A) interest rates increase

(B) interest rates decrease

(C) a person does not cash the bond when it matures

(D) the Federal Reserve decides to sell government securities

(E) the Federal Reserve decides to buy government securities

273. A bank's biggest asset is typically

(A) cash held in deposit
(B) loans made to customers
(C) real estate holdings
(D) goodwill and other intangibles
(E) local bonds

274. Because it is easier for a merchant to determine how much money to accept for a good or service than it is to determine the trade value of other goods offered as payment, money is useful as a

(A) medium of exchange
(B) store of value
(C) measure of value
(D) unit of account
(E) liquid source of wealth

275. The most liquid store of value would be

(A) a savings deposit
(B) a share of stock
(C) a Treasury bond
(D) a dollar bill
(E) a corporate bond

276. The M1 money supply includes

(A) traveler's checks
(B) bonds
(C) money market mutual funds
(D) common stocks
(E) preferred stocks

277. When a consumer decides to purchase a bond instead of holding cash, the consumer is giving up

(A) investment risk
(B) investment income
(C) liquidity
(D) protection from inflation
(E) a store of value

278. Bob deposits a roll of quarters into his savings account at the bank. How does this transaction affect the M1 and M2 money supply?

(A) M1 will decrease and M2 will decrease.
(B) M1 and M2 will remain the same.
(C) M1 will increase and M2 will decrease.
(D) M1 will remain the same and M2 will increase.
(E) M1 will decrease and M2 will remain the same.

279. Mike uses cash to purchase a bag of popcorn at a store. The store deposits the cash in its checking account. How does this transaction affect the M1 and M2 money supply?

(A) M1 will decrease and M2 will decrease.
(B) M1 and M2 will remain the same.
(C) M1 will increase and M2 will decrease.
(D) M1 will remain the same and M2 will increase.
(E) M1 will decrease and M2 will increase.

280. If the consumer price index fell by 75 percent, the purchasing power of the dollar would rise by

(A) 100 percent
(B) 200 percent
(C) 300 percent
(D) 400 percent
(E) 500 percent

281. Higher interest rates could be caused by

(A) an increase in the money supply
(B) a decrease in the money supply
(C) no change in the money supply
(D) a decrease in the demand for money
(E) no change in the demand for money

282. A decline in nominal interest rates could be caused by

(A) government deficit spending
(B) an increase in money demand
(C) an increase in the money supply
(D) a decrease in the money supply
(E) the central bank selling Treasury securities

283. Consumers will purchase more goods and services using credit if

(A) interest rates increase
(B) interest rates decrease
(C) the marginal propensity to save (MPS) increases
(D) the marginal propensity to consume (MPC) decreases
(E) interest rates do not change

284. If a borrower receives a loan from a commercial bank,

(A) bank liabilities are created
(B) bank assets are lost
(C) money is destroyed
(D) money is created
(E) interest rates decline

285. If the required reserve ratio is 20 percent and a commercial bank has $3 million in cash, $7 million on deposit at a Federal Reserve bank, and $2 million in government securities, it is allowed to lend out

(A) $12 million
(B) $10 million
(C) $8 million
(D) $4 million
(E) $2 million

286. If the required reserve ratio is 10 percent, and a commercial bank has the maximum amount of outstanding loans worth $18 million and $10 million on deposit at the Fed, its cash on hand is

(A) $18 million
(B) $20 million
(C) $10 million
(D) $8 million
(E) $2 million

287. If interest rates decrease, the result will be

(A) a decrease in the demand for money
(B) an increase in the amount of money demanded
(C) a decrease in the amount of money demanded
(D) an increase in the amount of money supplied
(E) a decrease in the amount of loans made by commercial banks

288. If Sherry deposits $500 in her checking account, and Robin pays back a loan for $4,000 to the bank, how will these transactions affect the supply of money?

(A) decrease by $3,500
(B) decrease by $4,000
(C) decrease by $4,500
(D) increase by $4,500
(E) increase by $4,000

289. When a commercial bank makes a loan to a borrower, the balance sheet of the bank

(A) shows a decrease in assets and an increase in liabilities
(B) shows an increase in assets and an increase in liabilities
(C) shows no change in assets and a decrease in liabilities
(D) shows an increase in assets and no change in liabilities
(E) shows a decrease in assets and no change in liabilities

290. If the reserve ratio is 20 percent, a $2,000 deposit at one bank can increase the money supply by as much as

(A) $2,000
(B) $1,600
(C) $400
(D) $10,000
(E) $8,000

291. If the reserve ratio is 25 percent, a $4,000 loan repayment at one bank can reduce the money supply by as much as

(A) $4,000
(B) $16,000
(C) $3,000
(D) $1,000
(E) $12,000

292. If the Federal Reserve wanted to increase the money supply, it could

(A) increase the reserve requirement
(B) leave the reserve requirement unchanged
(C) reduce the reserve requirement
(D) increase the discount rate
(E) cut income taxes

293. If the Federal Reserve wanted to reduce the money supply, it could

(A) reduce the reserve requirement
(B) leave the reserve requirement unchanged
(C) increase the discount rate
(D) reduce the discount rate
(E) raise income taxes

294. If the required reserve ratio is 20 percent, and a commercial bank has the maximum amount of outstanding loans at $32 million and $20 million in cash on hand, its assets at the Federal Reserve are

(A) $8 million
(B) $20 million
(C) $32 million
(D) $40 million
(E) $16 million

295. The maximum amount of money that can be added to the money supply when the central bank buys bonds from commercial banks is equal to the value of the bond purchase

(A) times the reserve ratio
(B) divided by the reserve ratio
(C) divided by the discount rate
(D) times the federal funds rate
(E) divided by the money multiplier

296. The money supply will increase by the value of the money multiplier times the value of the initial bank deposit when
- (A) the borrower does not deposit the full amount of the loan in a second bank
- (B) commercial banks do not loan out the maximum amount of money allowed by the Federal Reserve
- (C) the borrower keeps some of the loan money in currency instead of depositing it in the bank
- (D) commercial banks deposit a higher percentage of their funds at the Federal Reserve than they are required to
- (E) no money is held by the borrower or bank but rather loaned and redeposited

297. The Federal Reserve can increase the money supply by
- (A) selling government securities
- (B) purchasing government securities
- (C) increasing the discount rate
- (D) increasing the reserve requirement
- (E) increasing infrastructure spending

298. A shift of the money supply to the right was most likely caused by
- (A) the Federal Reserve selling government securities on the open market
- (B) the Federal Reserve buying government securities on the open market
- (C) the Federal Reserve increasing the discount rate
- (D) the Federal Reserve raising the reserve ratio
- (E) a decrease in government spending

299. A shift of the money supply to the right may be an attempt to
- (A) increase productivity
- (B) increase the current account surplus
- (C) reduce inflation
- (D) reduce the price level
- (E) stimulate the economy out of a recession

300. Which of the following would be a contractionary monetary policy?

    (A) selling government securities

    (B) buying government securities

    (C) increasing spending on government projects

    (D) increasing income taxes

    (E) decreasing income taxes

301. What is a benefit of expansionary monetary policy?

    (A) Aggregate demand will increase, but employment will decrease.

    (B) Aggregate demand will decrease, but employment will increase.

    (C) Aggregate demand will increase, and employment will increase.

    (D) Aggregate supply will increase, and employment will increase.

    (E) None of the above

302. Suppose the Federal Reserve increases the money supply and investment spending increases by $10 billion. What will happen to the aggregate demand if the MPC is 0.7?

    (A) increase by $33 billion

    (B) increase by $14 billion

    (C) decrease by $14 billion

    (D) decrease by $3 billion

    (E) increase by $3 billion

Use this scenario to answer questions 303 and 304: Joey sees an ad for a hamburger restaurant on television. The hamburger restaurant offers a gourmet burger for $10.

303. In this scenario, money is serving as a

    (A) store of value

    (B) unit of account

    (C) checkable deposit

    (D) money market mutual fund

    (E) medium of exchange

304. The hamburger restaurant collects the cash from the day's sales after it closes for the night and deposits it in the bank the next morning. In this scenario, money is serving as

(A) a store of value
(B) a unit of account
(C) M2 money
(D) a commodity currency
(E) a medium of exchange

305. How will a Treasury securities purchase by the central bank affect previously issued bonds?

(A) The price of bonds will remain unchanged.
(B) The price of bonds will fall.
(C) The price of bonds will rise.
(D) There is no connection to securities and bond prices.
(E) Banks will invest in more bonds.

306. The monetary policy most frequently used by central banks to offset a recession is/are

(A) raising taxes
(B) increasing the discount rate
(C) increasing the required reserve ratio
(D) open market operations
(E) raising interest rates

Refer to the following graph for questions 307 and 308.

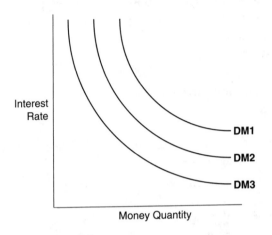

307. An increase in the demand for money can be caused by which of the following?
    (A) a decrease in the aggregate price level
    (B) banks eliminating interest-bearing checking accounts
    (C) a new application for your phone allowing you to use your phone as a debit card
    (D) consumption declining as a result of a recession
    (E) an increase in the rate of inflation

308. Why is the demand curve for money downward sloping?
    (A) It represents the relationship between the interest rate and the quantity of money.
    (B) It represents the relationship between the interest rate and the money supply.
    (C) It represents the relationship between the price level and the quantity of money.
    (D) It represents the relationship between the interest rate and the real GDP.
    (E) It represents the relationship between the price level and the real GDP.

Refer to the following graph for questions 309 and 310.

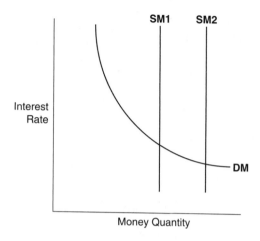

309. A shift in the money supply from SM1 to SM2 will cause
  (A) a decrease in the demand for money
  (B) an increase in the demand for money
  (C) no change in the interest rate
  (D) a decrease in the interest rate
  (E) an increase in the interest rate

310. If the money supply shifted from SM1 to SM2, the decision was made by
  (A) the Federal Reserve
  (B) mutual funds
  (C) multinational corporations
  (D) the federal government
  (E) commercial banks

311. If the required reserve ratio is 5 percent and a commercial bank has $10 million in cash, $30 million on deposit at a Federal Reserve bank, and $20 million in government securities, it is allowed to lend out
  (A) $30 million
  (B) $40 million
  (C) $38 million
  (D) $36 million
  (E) $28.5 million

Refer to the following graph for questions 312 and 313.

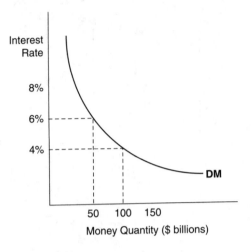

312. If the Federal Reserve increased the money supply from $50 billion
to $100 billion, the interest rate would

(A) increase to 6 percent
(B) fall to 6 percent
(C) fall to 4 percent
(D) increase to 4 percent
(E) increase to 8 percent

313. If the interest rate was at 8 percent, the money supply would be

(A) more than $150 billion
(B) $150 billion
(C) $100 billion
(D) $50 billion
(E) less than $50 billion

Refer to the following graph for questions 314 and 315.

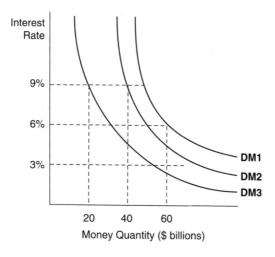

314. If the demand for money moved from DM1 to DM3 and the money supply was $60 billion, the interest rate would be
   (A) more than 9 percent
   (B) 9 percent
   (C) 6 percent
   (D) 3 percent
   (E) less than 3 percent

315. If the interest rate was 9 percent and demand for money moved from DM2 to DM3, the money supply would be
   (A) less than $20 billion
   (B) $20 billion
   (C) $40 billion
   (D) $60 billion
   (E) more than $60 billion

Long-Run Consequences of Stabilization Policies

316. Changes made to fiscal policy would involve changes in

(A) interest rates
(B) the reserve ratio
(C) the discount rate
(D) taxation
(E) open market operations

317. The original Phillips curve predicts that which situation cannot occur?

(A) inflation
(B) deflation
(C) stagflation
(D) recession
(E) full employment

318. When unemployment increases, the Phillips curve predicts

(A) an increase in inflation
(B) a decrease in inflation
(C) no change in inflation
(D) a decrease in aggregate supply
(E) a decrease in aggregate demand

319. The U.S. Congress lowered taxes to aid in the recovery from a recession. This is an example of

(A) the political business cycle
(B) contractionary fiscal policy
(C) discretionary fiscal policy
(D) nondiscretionary fiscal policy
(E) expansionary monetary policy

320. A decrease in aggregate demand would be caused by

(A) a contractionary fiscal policy
(B) no change in the price level
(C) an increase in aggregate supply
(D) a decrease in aggregate supply
(E) an expansionary fiscal policy

321. A set of fiscal policies that would counteract each other would be

(A) a decrease in government spending and no change in taxes
(B) an increase in government spending and no change in taxes
(C) a decrease in government spending and a decrease in taxes
(D) a decrease in government spending and buying government securities
(E) an increase in government spending and selling government securities

Refer to the following graph for questions 322 and 323.

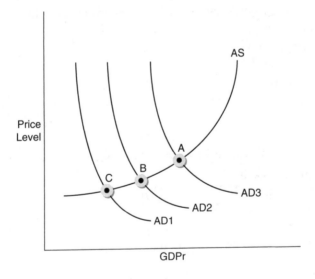

322. According to the graph, the economy is at equilibrium at Point A. Choose the best fiscal policy most appropriate to control demand-pull inflation.

(A) decrease aggregate demand by increasing taxes
(B) increase aggregate demand by decreasing taxes
(C) decrease aggregate supply by increasing taxes
(D) increase aggregate demand by increasing government spending
(E) decrease aggregate supply by selling government securities

323. According to the graph, the economy is also at equilibrium at Point B. Choose the best fiscal policy that would increase real GDP.

(A) increase aggregate demand from AD2 to AD1 by decreasing taxes
(B) decrease aggregate demand from AD2 to AD3 by increasing government spending
(C) decrease aggregate demand from AD2 to AD3 by decreasing government spending
(D) increase aggregate demand from AD2 to AD3 by decreasing taxes
(E) increase aggregate demand from AD2 to AD3 by buying government securities

324. Imagine the economy is in a recession. Which of the following fiscal policy suggestions would most likely be recommended?

(A) increase government spending or increase taxation
(B) increase government spending and decrease taxation
(C) increase government spending and increase taxation
(D) decrease government spending and decrease taxation
(E) A and B

325. If the U.S. government wanted to increase aggregate demand by $50 billion and the MPS is 0.4, then it should

(A) increase government spending by $20 billion
(B) increase government spending by $10 billion
(C) decrease government spending by $20 billion
(D) decrease government spending by $10 billion
(E) increase taxes by $20 billion

326. Because of automatic stabilizers, if income increases, government transfer spending

(A) increases and tax revenues decrease
(B) stays the same and tax revenues decrease
(C) stays the same and tax revenues increase
(D) decreases
(E) none of the above

327. What is often a result of full employment?

(A) The rate of inflation is zero.
(B) The MPS is 1.
(C) The MPC is 1.
(D) There is a balanced budget.
(E) Inflation increases.

328. The crowding-out effect refers to which of the following?

(A) Increases in government spending may raise the interest rate and reduce investment.
(B) Increases in government spending will shorten the recessionary gap.
(C) Decreases in consumption will increase taxes.
(D) High taxes reduce savings and decrease investment.
(E) High taxes increase savings and increase investment.

329. If the U.S. government adopts a fiscal policy that is

(A) expansionary, then net exports will likely increase
(B) expansionary, then net exports will likely decrease
(C) contractionary, then government securities will likely decrease
(D) contractionary, then government securities will likely increase
(E) none of the above

330. As a result of a progressive tax system, as income increases, the average tax rate will

(A) increase
(B) decrease
(C) increase at first and then gradually level off
(D) decrease at first and then gradually level off
(E) remain the same

331. Which fiscal policy would be the most contractionary?

(A) a $100 billion decrease in government spending
(B) a $100 billion increase in government spending
(C) a $100 billion decrease in taxes
(D) a $100 billion increase in taxes
(E) a $50 billion decrease in government spending and a $50 billion decrease in taxes

332. Suppose the U.S. economy is at potential GDP. If there is an increase in the money supply

(A) hyperinflation will result
(B) stagflation will result
(C) depreciation will result
(D) demand-pull inflation will result
(E) cost-push inflation will result

333. Cost-push inflation will occur if

(A) government regulation is decreased
(B) government spending is increased
(C) producers increase wages without gains in output
(D) there is an increase in investment spending
(E) B, C, and D

334. What happens to the Phillips curve in the long run?

(A) It will become vertical.
(B) It will become horizontal, intersecting the long-run aggregate supply curve.
(C) It will run parallel to the Laffer curve.
(D) It will run parallel to the short-run aggregate supply curve.
(E) A, C, and D

335. If the consumer price index increased by 33 percent, the purchasing power of the U.S. dollar fell by

(A) 25 percent
(B) 75 percent
(C) 100 percent
(D) 50 percent
(E) 125 percent

336. A recession is likely to occur if

(A) there is an increase in real GDP over a long period of time

(B) there is an increase in real GDP over a two-year period of time

(C) the government does not respond to demand-pull inflation with policy actions

(D) GDP falls for two consecutive quarters

(E) price levels remain constant and do not adjust to nominal GDP

337. The best explanation of the quantity theory of money would be

(A) that it measures the maximum amount of new checking deposits that can be created by a single dollar in excess reserves

(B) the interest rate paid on short-term loans

(C) nominal GDP is equal to the quantity of money

(D) the average number of times a dollar is spent in a year

(E) money supply times velocity equals price level times output

338. Mike is watching the news and hears the broadcaster say, "The government will begin to monetize the deficit." Curious about this statement, Mike asks his friend, who is an AP Economics teacher, about it. His friend explains that this statement means

(A) the Federal Reserve will buy government securities, which may result in inflation

(B) the Federal Reserve will print more money, which will decrease inflation

(C) the Federal Reserve will sell more government securities

(D) the Treasury will begin to repay the deficit

(E) the U.S. Congress will ask the Federal Reserve to increase the interest rate

339. Which situation might convince the Federal Reserve to pursue an expansionary fiscal policy?

(A) rising wages

(B) rising price level

(C) low cyclical unemployment

(D) high cyclical unemployment

(E) rising productivity

340. Which situation might convince the Federal Reserve to pursue a contractionary fiscal policy?

(A) falling wages

(B) falling price level

(C) rising price level

(D) high cyclical unemployment

(E) falling productivity

341. The equation for the quantity theory of money does NOT include

(A) money supply

(B) velocity of money

(C) money demand

(D) price level

(E) output

342. One advantage of monetary policy over fiscal policy is

(A) the speed at which it can be implemented

(B) the regulation of taxes and government spending

(C) the slow, methodical, and thoughtful pace at which it can be implemented

(D) its effectiveness on aggregate supply over aggregate demand

(E) A and B

343. The lending power of commercial banks decreases when

(A) central banks buy securities in the open market

(B) central banks sell securities in the open market

(C) the reserve ratio is decreased

(D) the U.S. Treasury collects increased income tax

(E) the Federal Reserve lowers the discount rate

344. If the Federal Reserve decided to pursue a contractionary policy, which actions would tend to offset each other?

(A) selling government securities and lowering the discount rate

(B) selling government securities and raising the discount rate

(C) buying government securities and lowering the discount rate

(D) selling government securities and raising the discount rate

(E) buying government securities and lowering the reserve ratio

345. Imagine the economy is experiencing high unemployment and a low rate of economic growth. What policy should the Federal Reserve follow?

(A) Pursue an easy money policy and sell government securities.
(B) Pursue a tight money policy and sell government securities.
(C) Pursue a tight money policy and buy government securities.
(D) Pursue an easy money policy and raise the reserve ratio.
(E) Pursue an easy money policy and buy government securities.

346. What happens to the money supply if the central bank pursues a contractionary monetary policy?

(A) It increases.
(B) It decreases.
(C) It remains the same.
(D) It equals full employment.
(E) It loses its value.

347. Suppose you read a *Wall Street Journal* article that states the Federal Reserve will lower the discount rate for the third time this year. According to this article, the Federal Reserve is trying to

(A) reduce inflation
(B) increase inflation
(C) stimulate the economy
(D) aid the U.S. Treasury
(E) increase checkable deposits

348. Suppose the economy is experiencing stable prices but high unemployment. Which monetary and fiscal policies would help reduce unemployment?

(A) purchase government securities and increase government spending
(B) purchase government securities and decrease government spending
(C) sell government securities and decrease government spending
(D) sell government securities and increase government spending
(E) purchase government securities and increase taxes

349. If the Federal Reserve buys $50 million in government securities, then the money supply will initially

(A) decrease by $50 million

(B) increase by $25 million

(C) increase by $50 million

(D) increase by $25 million and the purchasing power of commercial banks will increase by $25 million

(E) none of the above

350. The main purpose of expansionary monetary policy is to

(A) decrease aggregate demand

(B) increase aggregate demand

(C) increase aggregate supply

(D) decrease aggregate supply

(E) decrease investment spending

351. Demand-pull inflation refers to

(A) aggregate demand moving at a quicker pace than aggregate supply, thus an increase in price

(B) aggregate demand moving at a slower pace than aggregate supply, thus an increase in price

(C) an increase in prices brought on by a discovery of a new resource or new technology

(D) an increase in the price level from an increase in the cost of production

(E) the high cost of production being pushed onto the consumer

352. Cost-push inflation refers to

(A) an increase in the price level from an increase in the cost of production

(B) aggregate demand moving at a quicker pace than aggregate supply, thus an increase in price

(C) aggregate demand moving at a slower pace than aggregate supply, thus an increase in price

(D) an increase in prices brought on by a discovery of a new resource or new technology

(E) the increase in the price level due to hyperinflation

353. _____ fiscal policy tries to solve the problem of recession, whereas _____ fiscal policy tries to solve the problem of inflation.

(A) Expansionary, contractionary
(B) Contractionary, expansionary
(C) Tight, easy
(D) Expansionary, expansionary
(E) Contractionary, contractionary

354. The main purpose of a built-in stabilizer is to

(A) increase the government surplus during a recession without changing policy
(B) increase or decrease the government surplus without changing policy
(C) decrease the government surplus during inflation without changing policy
(D) increase or decrease the government surplus with a fast-pace change in policy
(E) bring the economy to full employment without changing policy

355. Built-in stabilizers are a part of

(A) discretionary fiscal policy
(B) discretionary monetary policy
(C) nondiscretionary monetary policy
(D) nondiscretionary fiscal policy
(E) balancing net imports and exports

356. A major problem or concern with fiscal policy is

(A) recognition lag
(B) inflation
(C) stagflation
(D) the swift pace at which it is implemented
(E) all of the above

357. Which of the following would be an advantage of automatic stabilizers?

(A) No additional policy or legislation is needed.
(B) They are more influential than discretionary fiscal policy.
(C) They always increase aggregate demand.
(D) They always increase aggregate supply.
(E) A and C

358. The Organization of Petroleum Exporting Countries (OPEC) dramatically increased the price of crude oil in 1973. The price of gasoline in the United States and around the world increased. This increase in price was

(A) hyperinflation
(B) deflation
(C) demand-pull inflation
(D) cost-push inflation
(E) none of the above

359. The main tools of the Federal Reserve are

(A) buying/selling securities, the discount rate, and increasing/decreasing taxes
(B) buying/selling securities, the reserve ratio, and increasing/decreasing taxes
(C) buying/selling securities, the discount rate, and the reserve ratio
(D) the discount rate, the reserve ratio, and increasing/decreasing taxes
(E) buying securities, the discount rate, and the reserve ratio

360. If the central bank decided to increase the discount rate, then it would be

(A) following contractionary monetary policy
(B) following expansionary monetary policy
(C) trying to sell government securities
(D) trying to buy government securities
(E) forcing banks to reserve more

361. Suppose there is a leftward shift in aggregate demand due to an increase in interest rates as a result of expansionary fiscal policy. This is known as

(A) the crowding-out effect
(B) an inflationary gap
(C) a recessionary gap
(D) cost-push inflation
(E) demand-pull inflation

362. If the Federal Reserve decreases the discount rate,

(A) it will be more difficult for commercial banks to borrow money
(B) it will contract the economy
(C) it will be easier for commercial banks to borrow money
(D) it is attempting to decrease inflation
(E) it is attempting to combat demand-pull inflation

363. If the Federal Reserve decided to lower the required reserve ratio, then this would

(A) contract the economy
(B) raise the price level
(C) lower the price level
(D) expand the economy
(E) decrease deposits

364. The average number of times per year a dollar is spent is known as

(A) the quantity theory of money
(B) cost-push inflation
(C) the velocity of money
(D) the capital account
(E) the rate of inflation

365. Changes made to monetary policy would include changes in

(A) the reserve ratio
(B) infrastructure spending
(C) tax policy
(D) the U.S. Constitution
(E) transfer payments

366. Which of the following illustrates an expansionary fiscal policy?

(A) an increase in taxation and an increase in government spending
(B) a decrease in taxation and a decrease in government spending
(C) a decrease in taxation and no change in government spending
(D) a decrease in taxation and an increase in government spending
(E) no change in taxation and an increase in government spending

367. The government reduces spending to cut its deficit. This is an example of

(A) expansionary fiscal policy
(B) contractionary monetary policy
(C) contractionary fiscal policy
(D) expansionary monetary policy
(E) decreasing taxes

368. An increase in aggregate demand would be implemented by

(A) an increase in aggregate supply
(B) an increase in taxation
(C) an increase in the discount rate
(D) an expansionary fiscal policy
(E) a contractionary fiscal policy

369. If the economy is experiencing demand-pull inflation, the government can counteract this with the fiscal policies of

(A) higher taxes and more government spending
(B) lower taxes and less government spending
(C) higher taxes and less government spending
(D) a higher reserve ratio
(E) lower taxes and more government spending

370. Demand-pull inflation would NOT be caused by

(A) worker expectations
(B) manufacturer expectations
(C) lower government spending
(D) an increase in exports
(E) an increase in private investment

371. A large increase in the money supply could cause

(A) a decrease in aggregate supply
(B) demand-pull inflation
(C) a decrease in aggregate demand
(D) a decrease in investment
(E) a decrease in the price level

372. Increasing government spending and reducing the tax rate would be the best policies for combating

(A) seasonal unemployment
(B) a rising price level
(C) structural unemployment
(D) cyclical unemployment
(E) inflation

373. If the government increased spending and raised taxes by equal amounts, the short-run effect would be

(A) an increase in inflation
(B) a decrease in inflation
(C) no change in the price level
(D) an increase in the price level
(E) a decrease in the price level

374. If the U.S. government wanted to increase aggregate demand by $100 billion and the MPS is 0.2, then it should

(A) increase government spending by $20 billion
(B) increase government spending by $80 billion
(C) decrease government spending by $80 billion
(D) increase taxes by $80 billion
(E) reduce government spending by $80 billion

375. If the U.S. government wanted to reduce aggregate demand by $50 billion and the MPS is 0.1, then it should

(A) increase government spending by $5 billion
(B) reduce government spending by $5 billion
(C) increase government spending by $10 billion
(D) increase government spending by $45 billion
(E) increase government spending by $50 billion

376. If the government decreased taxes, aggregate demand would

(A) shift to the left

(B) shift to the right

(C) remain unchanged

(D) cannot be answered without information about changes in government spending

(E) become vertical

377. If the government reduced spending, aggregate demand would

(A) shift to the right

(B) remain unchanged

(C) shift to the left

(D) cannot be answered without information about changes in the marginal tax rate

(E) become vertical

378. An automatic stabilizer would NOT include

(A) health care subsidies

(B) earned income tax credits

(C) rent subsidies

(D) corporate tax cuts

(E) grocery subsidies

379. A built-in stabilizer will be most effective when the marginal propensity to

(A) consume is low

(B) consume is high

(C) save is high

(D) import is high

(E) export is low

380. If the central bank pursues an expansionary policy, the money supply

(A) decreases

(B) increases

(C) remains the same

(D) cannot be determined without knowing the employment rate

(E) cannot be determined without knowing the tax rate

381. If the U.S. government adopts a fiscal policy that is

(A) contractionary, then net exports will likely increase
(B) contractionary, then net exports will likely decrease
(C) expansionary, then the reserve ratio will likely increase
(D) Expansionary, then government spending will likely decrease
(E) contractionary, then government spending will likely increase

382. Which fiscal policy would be the most expansionary?

(A) a $200 billion increase in taxes
(B) a $200 billion decrease in taxes
(C) a $100 billion decrease in taxes and a $100 billion increase in government spending
(D) a $200 billion increase in government spending
(E) a $200 billion decrease in government spending

383. A contractionary monetary policy is intended to

(A) reduce aggregate supply
(B) increase aggregate supply
(C) reduce aggregate demand
(D) increase aggregate supply
(E) increase exports

384. A decrease in GDP for two quarters is known as

(A) expansion
(B) stagflation
(C) recession
(D) equilibrium
(E) inflation

385. Which of the following would be an expansionary fiscal policy?

(A) increasing income taxes
(B) increasing transfer payments
(C) decreasing transfer payments
(D) increasing the discount rate
(E) decreasing the discount rate

386. Which of the following would be an expansionary monetary policy?

(A) increasing transfer payments
(B) decreasing taxes
(C) increasing government spending
(D) buying government securities
(E) selling government securities

387. What would be the result of contractionary monetary policy?

(A) Aggregate demand will increase and employment will decrease.
(B) Aggregate demand will increase and employment will increase.
(C) Aggregate demand and employment will both decrease.
(D) Aggregate demand and employment will both increase.
(E) Aggregate demand and employment will not change.

388. If there is an increase in federal tax rates, then it was caused by

(A) an increase in the money supply
(B) an expansionary fiscal policy
(C) the Federal Reserve
(D) the federal government
(E) the Securities and Exchange Commission

389. The lending power of commercial banks increases when

(A) central banks buy securities in the open market
(B) the reserve ratio increases
(C) tax receipts decrease
(D) the discount rate increases
(E) central banks sell securities in the open market

390. If the economy is experiencing cost-push inflation and is at full employment, how should the Federal Reserve act to reduce inflation?

(A) Pursue an easy money policy and buy government securities.
(B) Pursue an easy money policy and sell government securities.
(C) Pursue a tight money policy and reduce the reserve ratio.
(D) Pursue a tight money policy and sell government securities.
(E) Pursue an easy money policy and raise the reserve ratio.

391. If the Federal Reserve pursues an easy money policy, the money supply

    (A) decreases

    (B) increases

    (C) remains the same

    (D) cannot be determined without knowing the employment rate

    (E) cannot be determined without knowing the federal income tax rate

392. If the Federal Reserve is considering a discount rate hike, it may be trying to

    (A) stimulate the economy

    (B) reduce inflation

    (C) increase tax receipts

    (D) increase investment

    (E) reduce unemployment

393. If the Federal Reserve sells $80 million in government securities, the money supply will

    (A) increase by $80 million

    (B) decrease by $80 million

    (C) increase by $40 million

    (D) decrease by $40 million

    (E) remain unchanged

394. A tight money policy is intended to

    (A) reduce aggregate supply

    (B) increase aggregate supply

    (C) reduce aggregate demand

    (D) increase aggregate demand

    (E) increase exports

395. The lending power of commercial banks increases when

    (A) central banks sell securities in the open market

    (B) the reserve ratio is increased

    (C) the Federal Reserve lowers the discount rate

    (D) the U.S. government increases taxes

    (E) the U.S. government cuts infrastructure spending

396. Discretionary fiscal policies implemented in response to a recession would NOT include

(A) an increase in infrastructure investment

(B) a cut in income tax rates

(C) an decrease in corporate tax rates

(D) an increase in transfer payments

(E) a cut in social security contributions

397. If a recession occurs in a country with a progressive tax system,

(A) income tax receipts will fall slower than GDP

(B) income tax receipts will fall faster than GDP

(C) corporate tax receipts will fall slower than GDP

(D) transfer payments will decrease

(E) infrastructure spending will decrease

398. Automatic stabilizers include

(A) export tariffs

(B) property taxes

(C) auto registration fees

(D) health care subsidies

(E) direct taxes

399. The velocity of money has an inverse correlation with the

(A) discount rate

(B) unemployment rate

(C) income tax rate

(D) aggregate supply

(E) aggregate demand

400. The Federal Reserve can increase the velocity of money by

(A) increasing the money supply

(B) decreasing the money supply

(C) increasing taxes

(D) decreasing the price level

(E) decreasing exports

401. Two factors that would have opposite effects on the velocity of money would be

    (A) an increase in output and an increase in the price level
    (B) an increase in output and a decrease in the price level
    (C) an increase in output and a decrease in the money supply
    (D) an increase in the price level and a decrease in the money supply
    (E) an increase in the money supply and a decrease in output

402. Two factors that would have the same effect on the velocity of money would be

    (A) a decrease in output or an increase in the price level
    (B) an increase in the price level or an increase in money supply
    (C) a decrease in the price level or an increase in money supply
    (D) an increase in output or a decrease in the price level
    (E) a decrease in the price level or a decrease in money supply

403. The money supply in Nation X is $300 million. During the year, residents of Nation X spent $900 million on new goods and services. The velocity of money in Nation X is

    (A) 9
    (B) 12
    (C) 27
    (D) 3
    (E) 6

404. If technology advances increased the level of output in a country, and the money supply and price level did not change,

    (A) the velocity of money would not change
    (B) the velocity of money would increase
    (C) the velocity of money would decrease
    (D) aggregate demand would decrease
    (E) the discount rate would decrease

405. If a country had a money supply of $5 billion and a GDP of $20 billion, what is the velocity of money in this country?

(A) 5
(B) 4
(C) 15
(D) 25
(E) 100

406. If the velocity of money is 2 in a country, and the money supply is $300 million, what is the GDP of this country?

(A) $150 million
(B) $300 million
(C) $500 million
(D) $600 million
(E) $900 million

407. If a nation has a GDP of $600 million, and the velocity of money is 3, what is its money supply?

(A) $300 million
(B) $600 million
(C) $1.8 billion
(D) $1.2 million
(E) $200 million

408. Suppose a nation has a money supply of $150 million. If the velocity of money increases from 3 to 4,

(A) GDP will increase by $150 million
(B) GDP will increase by $600 million
(C) GDP will increase by $400 million
(D) GDP will decrease by $50 million
(E) GDP will decrease by $150 million

Refer to the following graph for questions 409 and 410.

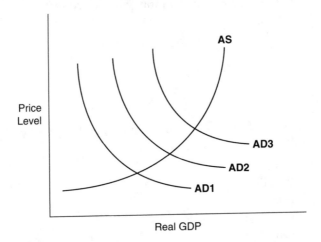

409. Suppose aggregate demand is at AD2 and a recession occurs. The goal of an automatic stabilizer would most likely be

(A) to shift aggregate demand from AD2 to AD3
(B) to shift aggregate demand from AD3 to AD2
(C) to shift aggregate demand from AD1 to AD2
(D) to shift aggregate demand from AD3 to AD1
(E) to keep aggregate demand stable at AD1

410. If aggregate demand was at AD2 and a recession occurred, and automatic stabilizers were not in place, it is likely that aggregate demand would

(A) remain stable at AD2
(B) shift from AD2 to AD3
(C) shift from AD2 to AD1
(D) shift from AD3 to AD2
(E) shift from AD1 to AD2

Refer to the following graph for questions 411 and 412.

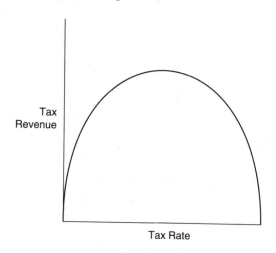

411. This graph depicts the
   (A) Phillips curve
   (B) Laffer curve
   (C) production possibilities curve
   (D) aggregate supply curve
   (E) aggregate demand curve

412. According to the Laffer curve, a tax cut could
   I. increase tax revenue
   II. decrease tax revenue
   III. have no effect on tax revenue
   IV. act as an automatic stabilizer
   (A) I only
   (B) II only
   (C) III only
   (D) I and II
   (E) IV only

Refer to the following graph of supply and demand for loanable funds for questions 413 and 414.

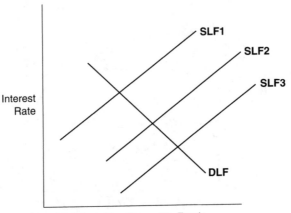

Quantity of Loanable Funds

413. If the government sold bonds to consumers to finance infrastructure investments, this could cause the supply of loanable funds to

(A) shift from SLF2 to SLF1
(B) shift from SLF1 to SLF2
(C) shift from SLF2 to SLF3
(D) remain stable at SLF2
(E) shift from SLF1 to SLF3

414. If the central bank sells bonds to finance the government's deficit spending for infrastructure investments, this could cause the supply of loanable funds to

(A) shift from SLF2 to SLF3
(B) shift from SLF2 to SLF1
(C) remain stable at SLF2
(D) shift from SLF1 to SLF2
(E) shift from SLF1 to SLF3

Refer to the following graph for questions 415 and 416.

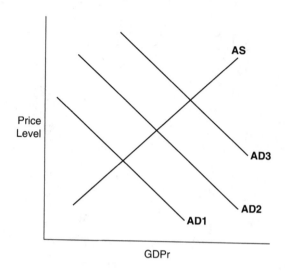

415. If real GDP is $40 billion, the government increases spending by $5 billion, and the spending multiplier is 4,
    (A) aggregate demand will shift from AD2 to AD3
    (B) aggregate demand will shift from AD1 to AD2
    (C) aggregate demand will shift from AD3 to AD2
    (D) the price level will increase from 100 to 150
    (E) the price level will decrease from 150 to 100

416. If real GDP is $60 billion, the government cuts spending by $20 billion, and the spending multiplier is 2,
    (A) aggregate demand will shift from AD2 to AD1
    (B) aggregate demand will shift from AD3 to AD2
    (C) aggregate demand will shift from AD3 to AD1
    (D) the price level will decrease from 150 to 100
    (E) the price level will increase from 100 to 150

Refer to the following graph for questions 417 and 418.

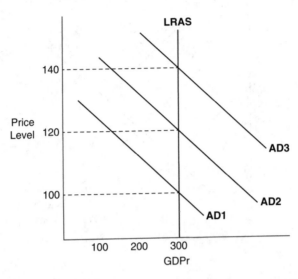

417. If the government increases spending, and aggregate demand moves from AD1 to AD2,
    (A) the price level increases from 100 to 140
    (B) the price level increases from 100 to 120
    (C) the price level increases from 120 to 140
    (D) real GDP increases from $200 billion to $300 billion
    (E) real GDP increases from $100 billion to $300 billion

418. The economy is at full employment when aggregate demand is on the
    I. AD1 curve
    II. AD2 curve
    III. AD3 curve

    (A) I only
    (B) II only
    (C) III only
    (D) II and III
    (E) I, II, and III

419. If the U.S. government wanted to increase aggregate demand by $20 billion and the MPC is 0.5, then it should

(A) increase government spending by $40 billion
(B) reduce government spending by $40 billion
(C) increase government spending by $20 billion
(D) increase government spending by $10 billion
(E) reduce government spending by $10 billion

420. If the U.S. government wanted to reduce aggregate demand by $40 billion and the MPC is 0.9, then it should

(A) increase government spending by $4 billion
(B) reduce government spending by $4 billion
(C) reduce government spending by $40 billion
(D) reduce government spending by $20 billion
(E) reduce government spending by $10 billion

421. An increase in per capita GDP

(A) correlates to an increase in the standard of living
(B) correlates to a decrease in the standard of living
(C) correlates to contractionary measures taken by the Federal Reserve
(D) correlates to a decrease in consumer investment
(E) correlates to a decrease in the labor force

422. GDP per capita refers to

(A) nominal GDP
(B) real GDP
(C) GNP
(D) GDP adjusted in inflationary terms
(E) GDP calculated per person

423. If an economy increased its output and there was no increase in the factors of production, it is said that

(A) technological progress occurred
(B) there was an increase in the labor force
(C) foreign imports decreased for that year
(D) more businesses used more capital but less labor
(E) more businesses used less capital but more labor

424. Economists calculate the standard of living in various nations by measuring

(A) GNP
(B) the debt-to-GDP ratio
(C) GDP
(D) the inflation rate
(E) GDP per capita

425. Derek works as a construction worker. Recently, he became certified to operate a large construction crane used to build skyscrapers. Economists would refer to this knowledge and skill as

(A) capital
(B) a scarce resource
(C) human capital
(D) capital stock
(E) technological progress

426. If there is an increase in capital stock, it will most likely lead to

(A) an increase in GDP and wages
(B) a decrease in GDP but not wages
(C) a decrease in GDP and wages
(D) an increase in wages but not GDP
(E) no change in GDP and wages

427. The president of the United States encourages Americans to help the economy grow in the long term. One suggestion would most likely be to

(A) buy imported goods
(B) increase consumption
(C) reduce immigration
(D) save and invest
(E) accumulate wealth

428. If the government wants to encourage growth within the economy, it would encourage

(A) consumers to buy imported goods
(B) investment in technological change
(C) an increase in taxes
(D) consumers to spend more money
(E) businesses to hire more workers

429. If there is a decrease in capital stock, this would result in

(A) no change in GDP and lower wages
(B) lower GDP and no change in wages
(C) lower GDP and lower wages
(D) higher GDP and higher wages
(E) no change in GDP or wages

430. If the government wanted to increase human capital, it should spend more money for

(A) infrastructure such as highways and telecommunications cables
(B) defense goods such as tanks and aircraft carriers
(C) public education
(D) law enforcement
(E) fire and flood prevention

431. If France has a GDP of $2 trillion and a population of 100 million, then the per capita GDP for France is

(A) $20,000
(B) $10,000
(C) $200,000
(D) $50,000
(E) $2,000

432. If per capita GDP is $40,000 in Italy, and the Italian GDP is $4 trillion, then the population of Italy is

(A) 40 million
(B) 400 million
(C) 100 million
(D) 1 billion
(E) 10 million

433. If the per capita GDP increases in the United States,

(A) the standard of living increases
(B) investment increases
(C) exports increase
(D) government spending increases
(E) the size of the workforce increases

434. Per capita GDP provides information about
- (A) income inequality
- (B) improvements in product quality
- (C) barter transactions
- (D) sustainability
- (E) the standard of living

435. If a new factory increases output in a country, per capita GDP increases by the
- (A) value of the output divided by the population
- (B) value of the output minus the population
- (C) cost of the output divided by the population
- (D) value of the wages paid divided by the increase in output
- (E) value of the output exported divided by the population

436. If the population of a country increases, but its total GDP does not change,
- (A) the standard of living will increase
- (B) the standard of living will not change
- (C) per capita GDP will decrease
- (D) per capita GDP will not change
- (E) per capita GDP will increase

437. If the population of a country remains the same and total GDP increases,
- (A) the standard of living will fall
- (B) the standard of living will increase
- (C) per capita GDP will decrease
- (D) per capita GDP will not change
- (E) the standard of living will not change

438. If the standard of living increases in a country and its population also increases,
- (A) per capita GDP decreases
- (B) there will be no change to GDP
- (C) total GDP increases
- (D) it is experiencing deflation
- (E) it is in a recession

439. If the Philippines has a GDP of $1 trillion and a population of 200 million, then the per capita GDP for the Philippines is

(A) $2,500

(B) $5,000

(C) $10,000

(D) $20,000

(E) $25,000

440. If per capita GDP in New Zealand increased from $25,000 to $30,000, while per capita GDP in Indonesia increased from $10,000 to $20,000, and the populations of both countries did not change,

(A) New Zealand grew more rapidly than Indonesia

(B) New Zealand's GDP increased by 15 percent

(C) Indonesia's GDP increased by 50 percent

(D) Indonesia grew more rapidly than New Zealand

(E) GDP per capita in New Zealand grew more rapidly than in Indonesia

CHAPTER 6

Open Economy—International Trade and Finance

441. An import quota on foreign cars would cause

(A) a decrease in GDP
(B) higher prices for consumers
(C) an increase in the total supply of cars
(D) lower prices for consumers
(E) an increase in GDP

442. Which of the following best describes the capital account on a nation's balance of payments?

(A) the current export payments of goods and services
(B) a limited amount of foreign currency
(C) the purchase of foreign real estate assets
(D) the sale of domestic real estate and financial assets
(E) the purchase and sale of real and financial assets between nations

443. Australia's economy is enjoying growth and expansion. How will this affect U.S. net exports, the value of the U.S. dollar, and the Australian dollar?

	U.S. Net Exports	Value of U.S. Dollar	Value of Australian Dollar
(A)	Decrease	Increase	Increase
(B)	Increase	Decrease	Increase
(C)	Decrease	Decrease	Increase
(D)	Increase	Increase	Increase
(E)	Increase	Increase	Decrease

444. If interest rates rise within a country,

(A) there is an increase in capital investment
(B) foreign tastes for this country's goods will increase
(C) there is a decrease in capital investment and an increase in financial investments
(D) there is a decrease in financial investments
(E) domestic financial investors will look to other countries to invest

445. A tariff refers to

(A) a prohibition against trading particular goods
(B) an elimination of trade with foreign nations
(C) the restriction on the sale of exports in another country
(D) a tax on imported goods
(E) the price difference between production cost and sale price

446. In a competitive market, nation XYZ produces bananas. Assuming there is free trade and the domestic price is higher than the world price, which of the following is true?

(A) There are no benefits to importing or exporting bananas.
(B) Nation XYZ will import bananas to eliminate a domestic surplus.
(C) Nation XYZ will export bananas to correct a domestic shortage.
(D) Nation XYZ will import bananas to correct a domestic shortage.
(E) Nation XYZ will export bananas to eliminate a domestic surplus.

447. Suppose the United States has a surplus balance in the current account. Which of the following statements is true?

(A) There is a balance of payments deficit.
(B) There was more foreign capital invested in the United States than there was U.S. investment abroad.
(C) There is a trade surplus.
(D) The United States sent more dollars abroad than there was foreign currency received.
(E) There is a trade deficit.

448. When the United States places an import quota on imported rice,

(A) consumers will buy rice substitutes
(B) consumers will use more rice and rice products
(C) the supply of rice decreases
(D) the United States will begin to export less rice
(E) makers of U.S. rice products suffer

449. Which of the following is a benefit of a protective tariff on imported timber?

(A) The domestic timber industry is made vulnerable to global competition.
(B) The domestic timber industry is protected from global competition.
(C) The price of foreign timber decreases.
(D) The United States consumes more foreign timber.
(E) There are no known benefits of a protective tariff.

450. Which of the following statements is false?

(A) Economic resources are reallocated toward inefficient producers.
(B) Lower consumer surpluses hurt consumers.
(C) Artificially high prices hurt consumers.
(D) Inefficient domestic producers are protected at the expense of foreign firms creating deadweight loss.
(E) Quotas collect revenue for the government.

451. If the U.S. dollar depreciates relative to the Chinese yuan, then

(A) U.S. goods sold in China would become cheaper
(B) U.S. goods sold in China would become more expensive
(C) more yuan are needed to buy a dollar
(D) prices would not differ for U.S. or Chinese goods
(E) none of the above

452. When the Japanese yen decreases in value relative to another currency, it has

(A) appreciated
(B) depreciated
(C) fixed
(D) floated
(E) inflated

453. Honda buys an automobile factory in Ohio. On the U.S. balance of payments this is recorded

(A) as outflow on U.S. assets abroad

(B) on the Official Reserves on the U.S. balance of payments

(C) as net investment income

(D) in the current account

(E) in the capital account as inflow of foreign assets to the United States

454. The law of comparative advantage states

(A) the more a nation produces of any one good, production costs rise

(B) the more a nation produces of any one good, production costs fall

(C) nations can mutually benefit from trade as long as the relative production costs differ

(D) all nations benefit from international trade

(E) all nations benefit from free trade

455. According to the theory of comparative advantage, a nation should

(A) produce and export goods that have low labor costs

(B) produce and export goods that have low monetary costs

(C) produce and export goods that have high labor costs

(D) produce and export goods that have low opportunity costs

(E) produce and export goods that have high opportunity costs

456. Currency exchange rates are determined by

(A) unregulated forces of supply and demand

(B) the federal government

(C) fiscal policies

(D) the balance between exports and imports

(E) protective tariffs

457. If the U.S. dollar increases in value as compared to a foreign currency, it is said that the U.S. dollar

(A) depreciated

(B) expanded

(C) shifted in value

(D) appreciated

(E) floated

458. The United States will have a trade surplus if

(A) the value of exports exceeds the value of imports
(B) the value of imports exceeds the value of exports
(C) there is a fixed exchange rate established by the U.S. Congress and not the market forces of supply and demand
(D) the market forces of supply and demand are allowed to set the exchange rate between two nations
(E) the U.S. dollar appreciates compared to a foreign currency

459. The difference between domestic price and world price is

(A) world prices are established above the equilibrium price
(B) domestic prices are usually below the world price equilibrium point
(C) domestic prices are used within a nation, and world prices are used between nations engaged in trade
(D) revenue tariffs are higher when nations engage in world prices
(E) revenue tariffs are lower when nations engage in world prices

460. The capital account refers to

(A) protective tariffs
(B) import quotas
(C) balance of payment
(D) the flow of investments between domestic and foreign nations
(E) the global equilibrium price of a good

461. The appreciation of a nation's currency relative to foreign currencies will

(A) increase that nation's exports
(B) decrease that nation's exports
(C) decrease that nation's exports and imports
(D) decrease tariffs
(E) increase the foreign exchange rate

462. A major argument for the North American free-trade zone was

(A) it would increase the loss of American jobs

(B) the United States, Canada, and Mexico would specialize according to comparative advantage

(C) the United States, Canada, and Mexico would not specialize according to comparative advantage

(D) North American nations wanted to compete with the European Union

(E) it would increase North American exports

463. One major example of economic integration in the Western Hemisphere in recent years is

(A) the European Union

(B) the World Trade Organization

(C) the North American Free Trade Agreement

(D) the Smoot-Hawley Act

(E) the Reciprocal Trade Agreements Act

464. When the U.S. dollar appreciates, it hurts

(A) an Englishman traveling to America

(B) an American traveling to a foreign country

(C) importers of goods and services

(D) fixed exchange rates

(E) competition among foreign competitors

465. When the U.S. dollar appreciates, it helps

(A) an Englishman traveling to America

(B) an American traveling to a foreign country

(C) exporters of goods and services

(D) fixed exchange rates

(E) competition among U.S. competitors

466. An import quota will result in

(A) decreased domestic employment

(B) an increase in domestic efficiency

(C) an increase in imports

(D) decreased protection for domestic producers

(E) an increase in domestic employment

467. When a country has a deficit in its balance of trade,

    (A) the value of its exports exceeds the value of its imports

    (B) the value of its imports exceeds the value of its exports

    (C) foreign investment in the country exceeds the value of its overseas investments

    (D) foreign investment in the country is less than the value of its overseas investments

    (E) the country is a net creditor to other countries

468. The current account deficit will NOT decrease as a result of

    (A) a decrease in imports

    (B) an increase in exports

    (C) a stronger domestic currency

    (D) a weaker domestic currency

    (E) an import tariff

469. If the Federal Reserve wanted to encourage foreign investors to invest capital in the United States, it could

    (A) decrease the discount rate

    (B) increase the discount rate

    (C) increase the reserve ratio

    (D) sell government securities

    (E) sell corporate bonds

470. If Brazil and Mexico are trading partners, and Mexico experiences a recession,

    (A) Mexico's imports from Brazil will increase

    (B) the Mexican peso will depreciate compared to the Brazilian real

    (C) the Mexican peso will appreciate compared to the Brazilian real

    (D) Brazil's exports to Mexico will increase

    (E) the Brazilian real will appreciate compared to the Mexican peso

471. If the Canadian dollar appreciates relative to the British pound, then

    (A) British goods sold in Canada would become more expensive

    (B) more Canadian dollars would be needed to buy a British pound

    (C) British goods sold in Canada would become less expensive

    (D) prices for goods in Britain and Canada would not change

    (E) Canada's exports to Britain would increase

472. If France produces cheese, and the price of cheese in France is lower than the price on the international market,

(A) France should export cheese to eliminate a domestic surplus
(B) France should import cheese to correct a domestic shortage
(C) France should import cheese to eliminate a domestic surplus
(D) France should export cheese to correct a domestic shortage
(E) France should not buy or sell cheese on the international market

473. If the United States removes a tariff on imported automobiles,

(A) the domestic automobile industry becomes vulnerable to foreign competition
(B) the domestic automobile industry receives protection from foreign competition
(C) jobs in the domestic automobile industry will increase
(D) imported automobiles will become more expensive
(E) the price of imported automobiles will not change

474. If the United States places an import quota on foreign sugar,

(A) the price of sugar in the United States will decrease
(B) consumers in the United States will purchase more sugar
(C) consumers in the United States will purchase less sugar
(D) domestic sugar producers will hire fewer workers
(E) consumers in the United States will purchase fewer sugar substitutes

475. Remittances from international workers are included in

(A) the balance of trade
(B) net factor income
(C) net cash transfers
(D) the capital account
(E) foreign direct investment

476. If Hong Kong removes the currency peg from the Hong Kong dollar, the Hong Kong dollar is

(A) appreciated
(B) depreciated
(C) fixed
(D) floated
(E) inflated

477. If the Swedish kroner has a constant exchange value in comparison to the euro, the Swedish kroner is

(A) appreciated
(B) depreciated
(C) fixed
(D) floated
(E) inflated

478. If Canada removes a tariff on imported lumber,

(A) economic resources are allocated toward more efficient lumber companies
(B) consumer surplus decreases
(C) lumber prices increase
(D) the Canadian government collects more tax revenue
(E) lumber imports decrease

479. If Honda sells a motorcycle factory in California, this is recorded

(A) as inflow on U.S. assets abroad
(B) in the capital account as outflow of foreign assets from the United States
(C) on the Official Reserves on the U.S. balance of payments
(D) as net investment income
(E) in the current account

480. If a customs agency requires a firm to submit complicated forms and filings before allowing the firm to import goods, this is

(A) a tariff
(B) a quota
(C) a non-tariff trade barrier
(D) an embargo
(E) free trade

481. When a foreign country sells goods in the United States for less than production costs, this is

(A) comparative advantage
(B) dumping
(C) free trade
(D) absolute advantage
(E) a cartel

482. A nation's options to deal with dumping would NOT include

(A) a tariff
(B) a quota
(C) free trade
(D) an embargo
(E) a non-tariff trade barrier

483. If a U.S. dollar is initially worth 60 Indian rupees, and the exchange rate fluctuates so a U.S. dollar is worth 90 Indian rupees,

(A) the rupee appreciated 50 percent
(B) the U.S. dollar appreciated 50 percent
(C) the U.S. dollar depreciated 50 percent
(D) the U.S. dollar appreciated 100 percent
(E) the rupee depreciated 100 percent

484. If a U.S. dollar is worth 20 Mexican pesos, and the exchange rate fluctuates so a U.S. dollar is worth 10 Mexican pesos,

(A) the U.S. dollar depreciated 50 percent
(B) the U.S. dollar depreciated 20 percent
(C) the U.S. dollar appreciated 100 percent
(D) the Mexican peso appreciated 50 percent
(E) the Mexican peso depreciated 50 percent

485. A strong U.S. dollar policy would create

(A) increased tourism revenue
(B) low domestic interest rates
(C) an increase in imports
(D) an increase in exports
(E) lower domestic unemployment

486. A weak U.S. dollar policy would result in

(A) high domestic interest rates
(B) increased tourism revenue
(C) increased domestic unemployment
(D) less competitive exports
(E) an increase in imports

487. If foreign investors believed that the Federal Reserve planned to leave the discount rate unchanged,

(A) the value of the U.S. dollar would increase
(B) the value of the U.S. dollar would decrease
(C) U.S. imports would become less expensive
(D) U.S. imports would become more expensive
(E) U.S. imports would stay the same

488. A weak U.S. dollar helps

(A) domestic businesses that import goods
(B) the foreign exchange rate
(C) overseas manufacturers
(D) domestic businesses that export goods
(E) American tourists

489. If the Australian central bank raises the discount rate while the Federal Reserve leaves its discount rate unchanged,

(A) the Australian dollar will depreciate against the U.S. dollar
(B) the Australian dollar will appreciate against the U.S. dollar
(C) Australian exports to the United States will increase
(D) American tourism to Australia will increase
(E) American imports from Australia will increase

490. If the Canadian central bank cuts the discount rate and the Federal Reserve raises the discount rate,

(A) American tourism to Canada will decrease
(B) Canadian exports to the United States will decrease
(C) the Canadian dollar will appreciate against the U.S. dollar
(D) American exports to Canada will increase
(E) American imports from Canada will increase

491. If American demand for Brazilian sugar increased,

(A) the U.S. dollar would appreciate against the Brazilian Real
(B) the Brazilian Real would appreciate against the U.S. dollar
(C) the Brazilian central bank would raise the discount rate for the Real
(D) the Federal Reserve would raise the discount rate for the U.S. dollar
(E) the exchange rate for the U.S. dollar compared with the Brazilian Real would not change

492. If the Argentinian economy was experiencing inflation,

(A) the U.S. dollar would depreciate against the Argentinian peso

(B) the exchange rate for the U.S. dollar compared to the Argentinian peso would not change

(C) the U.S. dollar would appreciate against the Argentinian peso

(D) the Federal Reserve would raise the discount rate for the U.S. dollar

(E) tourism from Argentina to the United States would increase

493. If the French government places a tariff on imported cars,

(A) consumer surplus increases

(B) car prices decrease

(C) the French government collects more tax revenue

(D) car imports increase

(E) economic resources are allocated toward more efficient car manufacturers

494. If investors believed that the New Zealand central bank planned to cut the discount rate,

(A) the value of the New Zealand dollar would increase

(B) the value of the New Zealand dollar would stay the same

(C) the value of the New Zealand dollar would decrease

(D) New Zealand exports would become less expensive

(E) New Zealand imports would decrease

495. An increase in supply for the Norwegian kroner will cause

(A) a decrease in kroner demand

(B) a decrease in Norwegian exports

(C) kroner depreciation

(D) kroner appreciation

(E) an increase in Norwegian imports

496. An increase in demand for the Russian ruble will cause

(A) ruble depreciation

(B) ruble appreciation

(C) an increase in ruble supply

(D) an increase in Russian exports

(E) a decrease in Russian imports

497. The South Korean government decides to protect its domestic auto market by limiting the number of cars imported from China. This is an example of a(n)

(A) embargo
(B) quota
(C) tariff
(D) free trade agreement
(E) currency devaluation

498. Chile, Argentina, Peru, and Bolivia reach agreement on a treaty to eliminate tariffs for goods exchanged between their countries. This is an example of a

(A) common currency
(B) free trade agreement
(C) balance of trade
(D) currency devaluation
(E) trade war

499. The U.S. dollar is initially worth 150 Japanese yen. If the exchange rate fluctuates and the U.S. dollar is now worth 100 Japanese yen, the Japanese yen

(A) appreciated by 33 percent
(B) appreciated by 50 percent
(C) appreciated by 67 percent
(D) depreciated by 50 percent
(E) depreciated by 33 percent

500. The U.S. dollar is initially worth three Brazilian reals. If the exchange rate fluctuates and the U.S. dollar is now worth six Brazilian reals, the Brazilian real

(A) depreciated by 50 percent
(B) depreciated by 67 percent
(C) depreciated by 33 percent
(D) appreciated by 50 percent
(E) appreciated by 100 percent

ANSWERS

Chapter 1: Basic Economic Concepts

1. (A) Macroeconomics is the study of aggregate indicators within an economy, as well as fiscal and monetary policies and their outcomes. It does not concentrate on the individual companies and individuals in the economy; that is microeconomics.

2. (A) Choice (A) is the best answer because Line A represents a supply curve, which is upward sloping. Choices (B), (C), and (D) are incorrect because they are downward sloping, which indicates a demand curve.

3. (B) Specialization and gains from trade should cause the standard of living within a country to increase. If trade does not benefit both countries involved, the trade is not likely to occur.

4. (A) Choice (A) is correct. The key to understanding comparative advantage is to understand opportunity cost. If a producer can make a good at a lower opportunity cost than all other producers, it is said that the producer has a comparative advantage. Choices (B), (C), and (D) do not incorporate opportunity cost; therefore, they are incorrect.

5. (C) Specialization and trade based on comparative advantage allow economies to consume beyond their production possibilities curve through mutually beneficial gains from trade.

6. (E) Trade will exist between two countries if there is a comparative advantage between the two countries or each country is producing its good at a lower opportunity cost than the other. Choice (A) would certainly be good for both countries, but the question asks when it is truly beneficial for two countries to trade with each other. Choice (B) is incorrect because it refers to a decrease in production costs as output increases, which does not factor into trade between two countries. Choice (C) is the opposite of Choice (B) and still has nothing to do with trade between two countries. Choice (D) is incorrect because absolute advantage refers to the ability to produce more of a good than all other producers.

7. (A) The production possibilities curve represents the maximum output between two goods. It also reflects the opportunity costs between these two goods because resources are scarce. Any point along the curve is the maximum output producing both of the goods and therefore is an attainable and efficient use of resources. Choices (B) and (C) do not reflect this maximum output. Choice (D) is incorrect because this would be represented by a point inside the production possibilities curve, not on it.

8. (A) Choice (A) is correct. This is the best answer because in economics, "growth" is always represented by a rightward movement of any curve on any graph. Choices (B) and (C) are incorrect because they reflect movement along the curve, not the movement of the curve itself. Choice (D) is incorrect because the intersection of the supply and demand curves is the equilibrium point where price is usually set. Choice (E) is incorrect because it is unrelated to economic growth.

9. (C) The production possibilities curve represents the maximum output between two goods using scarce resources. As such, it represents the opportunity costs incurred when the production shifts to more of one product than the other. The more a producer chooses to make of a product, the more the opportunity costs increase for the product not being produced. Choice (A) is incorrect because it reflects the opposite idea of a production possibilities curve. Choice (B) is incorrect because a production possibilities curve reflects only the production combination of two goods, not taxes.

10. (A) Choice (A) is the best answer because an opportunity cost is the most profitable alternative given up when you make a decision; Tommy could have earned $20 tutoring his brother for two hours. Choices (B) and (C) are incorrect because the question does not ask for the marginal benefits and marginal costs. Choice (D) is incorrect because Tommy is giving up the chance to earn $20, so it would never be an opportunity cost of zero.

11. (C) Choice (C) is the best answer because it best represents the concept of opportunity cost. Choices (A) and (B) are incorrect because they represent only the costs incurred while building the performing arts center, not the next best alternative.

12. (A) Choice (A) is correct. Discovery of a new resource is a fundamental factor that results in economic growth. Economic growth is represented by a rightward shift of the production possibilities curve. Since Tanen found the resource, it would affect only its curve and not Reilly's. Choices (C) and (D) are incorrect because a leftward shift indicates a contracting economy.

13. (D) Choice (D) is correct. If a market overallocates its resources, quantity supplied will be more than the allocatively efficient quantity.

14. (B) Choice (B) is correct. Government ownership of the factors of production exists under a command economy, not in a market economy. A market economy is based on the freedom of the market forces of supply and demand.

15. (E) Choice (E) is correct. The production possibilities curve represents the maximum output between two goods using scarce resources. Choice (A) represents the relationship between tax rates and government revenue. Choice (B) represents the relationship between inflation and unemployment. Choice (C) is incorrect because the equilibrium point represents the price level. Choice (D) is incorrect because it represents where marginal costs increase as one additional unit of product is produced.

16. (E) In microeconomics and macroeconomics, the idea of scarcity always juxtaposes human beings' unlimited wants with limited natural resources. Choice (E) is the best answer. All other choices do not reflect this relationship.

17. (C) Choice (C) is the best answer because it best reflects the idea of comparative advantage. If a producer can make a good at a lower opportunity cost than all the other producers, it is said that he has a comparative advantage. Luca can weed the garden at a lower opportunity cost than Sarah, so it would be mutually beneficial if he weeded the garden and Sarah walked the dog.

18. (D) If the current market price is higher than the equilibrium market price, it causes the quantity supplied to be higher than the quantity demanded. This results in a surplus. That surplus causes producers with the market to decrease their prices to eliminate their surpluses.

19. (A) Choice (A) is the best answer because the difference between supply and aggregate supply is the basic difference between microeconomics and macroeconomics. Supply is used in microeconomics to represent the total amount of a good available to consumers for an individual market; for example, the supply of apples. Aggregate supply is used in macroeconomics to represent the total supply of all goods in an economy, where the supply level is represented for an entire country.

20. (A) Factors of production are resources that go into producing goods and services. Choice (A) is correct because these are fundamental resources needed to produce goods and services. Land, labor, and capital are identified as factors of production.

21. (D) An outward shift represents economic growth. The best answer would be an element that adds to the growth of the economy. Choice (D) is the best answer because an increase in skilled workers would increase production. Choices (A), (B), and (C) would cause the production possibilities curve to shift to the left.

22. (C) Choice (C) is correct. It is translated as "holding other things constant," or "all else equal." This term is used in economics to help describe the effect a variable might have on other economic factors. If other things are not equal, then a variety of factors may change the outcome of an economic decision.

23. (B) Choice (B) is correct. Specialization refers to the production of goods based on comparative advantage. If a nation can produce a good at a lower opportunity cost, then it would be beneficial if it specialized in producing that good and traded with another nation that specialized in producing other goods. Consuming more than the production possibilities curve necessitates specialization and trade. Choices (C), (D), and (E) are incorrect because they are factors that shift the production possibilities curve to the right.

24. (A) Choice (A) is the best answer because it talks about the opportunity cost. The production possibilities curve represents the opportunity cost. Choice (B) is incorrect because vital resources are always scarce. Choice (C) is incorrect because that would be a point inside the production possibilities curve. Choices (D) and (E) are incorrect because the production possibilities curve does not reflect marginal utility or benefit.

25. (C) Choice (C) is correct. In the most general sense, the more a good or service costs, the less people are willing and able to pay for it. This idea is an inverse, or indirect, relationship graphically represented as a downward sloping curve. Choices (A) and (B) are incorrect because price will not shift the entire demand curve to the right or the left. Choice (D) is incorrect because complementary goods are used alongside other goods, like tennis balls and tennis rackets. Choice (E) is incorrect because it refers to a direct relationship.

26. (A) Choice (A) is correct. In a market system, resources are allocated through the decisions of firms and consumers. Price is therefore determined through the equilibrium point between supply and demand. Choice (B) is incorrect because it reflects the operation of a command economy. Choice (C) is incorrect because opportunity cost does not influence how prices are determined; rather it is the cost based on the value of the next best alternative. Choice (D) is incorrect because more information is needed, such as the amount producers are willing to produce at each price level. Choice (E) is incorrect because the Fed cannot set the price level.

27. (E) Cotton T-shirts and shirts made of other fabrics are substitutes for each other. As a result, any increase in the price of one will cause consumers to demand more of the other at all prices. This shifts the demand curve for that product to the right.

28. (B) Choice (B) is the best answer because bowling shoes are complementary goods. If a good shows an increase in demand, then all of its complements will show an increase in demand. This is so because if the demand for bowling balls increases, more people are bowling, and therefore, more people will also need bowling shoes.

29. (B) Choice (B) is correct. When the market is left to itself without any government regulations, such as price floors or ceilings, the market price is established at the equilibrium point between supply and demand.

30. (A) Terms of trade are the quantities used for the mutual benefit of both economies within the international market. The opportunity cost for both countries determines what the mutually beneficial terms of trade will be.

31. (B) As the number of consumers within the market increases, the demand for tacos will also increase, or move to the right, causing the price within the market to rise.

32. (C) The determinants of supply are: natural and manmade phenomenon, input prices, competition, expected prices, joint production costs, alternate production costs, government taxes and subsidies, and technology. The income of consumers would influence the demand for a product, not the supply.

33. (A) Choice (A) is correct.

34. (D) Terms of trade are the quantities used for the mutual benefit of both economies within the international market. The opportunity cost for both countries determines what the mutually beneficial terms of trade will be. If the terms of trade are mutually beneficial, both countries will agree to trade.

35. (E) Country X's opportunity cost of producing wheat is ¼ of a car (100/400). They will therefore only accept ¼ or more of a car in order to trade for 1 bushel of wheat.

36. (C) Choice (C) is correct because consumption will rise in both countries.

37. (B) Choice (B) is correct. A point inside the production possibilities curve is attainable but not efficient because output of both goods could be greater.

38. (A) A recession is characterized by high unemployment. This means that a resource is not being used to its full potential. When this occurs, current production is found to be inside the maximum possible production, or inside the PPC.

39. (C) Choice (C) is the best answer. A production possibilities curve is concave because of specialization, but if a nation's resources are not specialized the production possibilities curve will be flat.

40. (B) Choice (B) is the best answer. Specialized resources will result in increasing opportunity costs.

41. (D) Choice (D) is the best answer because it represents the decision to give up other goods and services.

42. (C) Choice (C) is the best answer. Saudi Arabia's production capacity would fall, and the production possibilities curve would shift to the left, while Russia's production capacity would not change.

43. (C) Any point that is located ON the production possibilities curve is at full employment. Any point inside the production possibilities curve shows unemployed resources.

44. (C) Golf balls and rounds of golf are direct complements. You require golf balls in order to play a round of golf. Therefore, if the price of a round of golf declines, you will demand a higher quantity of golf balls at all prices. This is shown by a movement of the demand for golf balls from Line B to C.

45. (D) Golfing and bowling are direct substitutes. You do not require golf balls in order to bowl. Therefore, if more people are bowling than golfing, the market will demand a lower quantity of golf balls at all prices. This is shown by a movement of the demand for golf balls from Line B to D.

46. (C) Choice (C) is the best answer. To achieve allocative efficiency, a nation must have full employment.

47. (E) If the opportunity cost of producing the aircraft carriers for France declines to below what they can trade with the United States, they will choose to produce them domestically.

48. (A) Choice (A) is the best answer because labor is a factor of production.

49. (A) Choice (A) is the best answer. A society must use limited resources to produce the goods consumers demand.

50. (C) Choice (C) is correct. A production possibilities curve only shows output for two different goods, which is a major simplification of a nation's economy.

51. (B) Choice (B) is the best answer. The other choices would make higher output possible.

52. (A) Choice (A) is correct. Increased trade allows each country to specialize, allowing increased consumption. Both countries benefit from trade, but their production possibilities curves will not change.

53. (C) A bowed-out production possibilities curve represents an increasing opportunity cost for both goods. Therefore, increasing sugar production will decrease car production at ever increasing rates.

54. (B) A linear (straight line) production possibilities curve represents a constant opportunity cost between both goods. Therefore, increasing bread production will decrease cake production at constant rates.

55. (B) Choice (B) is the best answer, as this is the law of demand.

56. (A) The interaction of supply and demand within a market creates an equilibrium price and quantity where supply and demand cross. This represents the point at which quantity demanded meets quantity supplied, creating a market price.

57. (C) Choice (C) is the best answer. All of the other choices involve a government making market decisions.

58. (A) Steve produces more of each computers and bicycles than Todd and so has absolute advantage in both goods. However, his opportunity cost of production is only lower than Todd's for bicycles, and so he also has a comparative advantage for bicycles.

59. (C) All things are scarce, causing decisions to be made for the best use of resources. A shortage of a good or service occurs when there is excess demand or not enough supply for those items.

60. (A) Choice (A) is correct. A country with an absolute advantage can produce more of a good than another country. Trade will still benefit both countries if a comparative advantage is present.

61. (D) The interaction of supply and demand for a good or service represents a market creating an equilibrium price and quantity where supply and demand cross.

62. (E) Choice (E) is the best answer. Production capacity affects supply, not demand.

63. (B) Choice (B) is the best answer. Consumer tastes affect demand, not supply.

64. (A) Choice (A) is correct as this statement describes the income effect.

65. (E) If this country wants to experience greater growth, it should move production from Point A to Point B. The movement to create a larger quantity of capital goods than consumer goods allows for increased possible production and therefore a greater chance for growth. The movement from Point A to Point E is impossible with given resources and without trade.

66. (A) If this country wants to produce at the best possible place, it should produce at Point A, B, or C. Any of these represents the most efficient use of their resources. Point D is an inefficient use of resources. Point E is impossible with given resources and without trade.

67. (B) Point D represents a recession within this economy. As this economy moves out of a recession, its efficient use of its resources increases and moves toward the production possibilities curve. This is shown as a movement from Point D to Point A.

68. (B) Equilibrium is represented by Point A, as it is the point at which quantity supplied is equal to quantity demanded.

69. (A) A shortage occurs when the quantity supplied (Point D) is lower than the quantity demanded (Point E) and is always below the market equilibrium price and quantity (Point A).

70. (C) A surplus occurs when the quantity supplied (Point C) is higher than the quantity demanded (Point B) and is always above the market equilibrium price and quantity (Point A).

Chapter 2: Economic Indicators and the Business Cycle

71. (E) Choice (E) is the best answer because it states that workers, entrepreneurs, and owners of capital all offer their services through a resource market (a market used to exchange the services of resources of land, labor, and capital). A product market in choice (A) refers to the mechanism used to exchange goods and services. The circular flow model also incorporates the role of the government and the foreign sector.

72. (A) In the circular flow model, households serve as the buyers of finished products and the sellers of resources. Businesses are the buyers of resources and the sellers of finished products. Choice (A) would be the best answer. Choices (B), (D), and (E) are incorrect because businesses are sellers of products and demanders of resources. Choice (C) is incorrect because GDP is calculated through either the income or expenditure approach.

73. (A) Choice (A) is correct. The circular flow model shows how households, individuals, and businesses circulate resources, goods, and income throughout the economy.

74. (A) Choice (A) is correct. The GDP refers to all final goods produced in an economy for a one-year period. Intermediate goods are not counted in the GDP, to avoid double counting. Choice (D) is incorrect because the GDP does not calculate domestic businesses in foreign locations, so a McDonald's located in London, England, would be left out. Choice (E) is incorrect because it is only half of the equation to calculate GDP.

75. (C) Choice (C) is correct because GDP does not include income from domestic businesses operating in foreign countries.

76. (E) GDP does not count for non-market and black-market transactions. It also does not account for happiness, leisure time, volunteerism, or quality increases.

77. (A) Choice (A) is correct. A leakage in the circular flow model is anything that would decrease the consumption of goods and services. Taxes would decrease a consumer's purchasing power and a firm's production output. The same goes for an individual's or household's savings.

78. (C) Intermediate goods are not counted in the GDP, to avoid double counting. A computer chip, lumber, and a used car would succumb to double counting if they were calculated into the GDP. So the best answer would be Choice (C), a new car.

79. (B) Choice (B) is correct. Households own the factors of production, or resources, in the circular flow model.

80. (A) Intermediate goods are added to the final calculation of GDP as a part of the whole good that they make up. This allows for a single counting of the cumulative value of the good, rather than counting BOTH the parts AND the whole of that good, and avoids double counting.

81. (D) Choice (D) is correct. You must know the formula for calculating GDP: C + I + G + (X – M). C represents consumer spending; I represents private investments; G represents government spending and government investments; X represents exports; and M represents imports. Savings are not calculated into the GDP.

82. (A) Choice (A) is correct. The circular flow model is often expanded to illustrate the role government plays in the distribution of goods and services throughout the economy. If the government is added into the circular flow model, it indicates it is participating in providing goods and services to businesses and households.

83. (E) You must know the formula for calculating GDP: C + I + G + (X – M). Choice (E) is the best answer, whereas Choices (A), (B), (C), and (D) would represent miscalculations.

84. (C) Choice (C) is correct. Although Jason and Mary take out a loan and spend a significant portion of their savings on the purchase of a new home, this would be calculated as an investment. Purchase of real estate, such as a house or a condominium, would be calculated in the GDP as investment because all homeowners want their properties to increase in value and see a positive return if they choose to sell the house in the future.

85. (B) The initial change in GDP would be equal to the initial amount of investment ($150 billion) subtracted from the final total of investment ($250 billion). $250 – $150 = $100 billion increase in investment, and therefore a $100 billion increase in initial GDP.

86. (A) Choice (A) is correct. GDP = C (1,000) + I (350) + G (600) + (X – M) (150 – 175) = $1,925.

87. (B) Nominal GDP is defined as the value of production at current prices, whereas real GDP is the value of production using prices at a fixed point in time. Choice (B) is the best answer because it explains a change in value over time.

88. (A) Choice (A) is correct. If the price index is less than 100, real GDP is greater than nominal GDP.

89. (E) Choice (E) is correct. The labor force is defined as all individuals 16 years and older who are currently employed or unemployed. People who are not actively looking for work are not considered part of the labor force.

90. (A) Choice (A) is correct. The labor force is defined as all individuals 16 years and older who are currently employed or unemployed. People who are not actively looking for work are not considered part of the labor force.

91. (B) Choice (B) is correct. Frictional unemployment is created through turnover in the labor market, or when existing workers leave their jobs to look for better ones.

Elaine quitting her job to go back to school and look for a better job places her as frictionally unemployed.

92. (A) Choice (A) is correct. Cyclical unemployment occurs when there are too few jobs due to an economic downturn. If structural and frictional unemployment are at a minimum and cyclical unemployment is zero, it is said the economy is approaching full employment.

93. (B) Choice (B) is correct. The consumer price index measures changes in the price level of consumer goods and services. The producer price index measures average changes in the price level of produced goods by producers. Calculating changes in the price levels for consumer goods and the output by producers, economists have a better understanding of the rate of inflation.

94. (C) Choice (C) is correct. Stagflation occurs in the macro-economy when inflation and the unemployment rate are both increasing. Real GDP is also decreasing at this time. This is also known as cost-push inflation.

95. (A) Choice (A) is correct. Cyclical unemployment occurs when there are too few jobs due to an economic downturn.

96. (E) The calculation for unemployment is the number of unemployed workers divided by the labor force multiplied by 100. In this case the calculation would be $(1,000/9,000) \times 100 = 11\%$.

97. (B) Choice (B) is correct. Remember, the labor force does not calculate the number of people not working. The labor force is defined as all individuals 16 years and older who are currently employed or unemployed. People who are not actively looking for work are not considered part of the labor force.

98. (A) Choice (A) is correct. The firm sold 90 bicycles and inventory increased by 20 bicycles (120 – 100), so output was 110 bicycles. These bicycles were worth $50 each, so output was $5,500.

99. (B) The consumer price index measures the average price level using a base year. It is the best measure of consumer inflation. Choice (B) would be the best answer if one were to check the rate of inflation in the economy.

100. (B) Inflation takes away purchasing power of income and assets. All of the examples except B are losing value, as they do not account for changes in prices (inflation). In B, any change in price (inflation) would be offset by the cost-of-living increase, making sure to keep up with the unexpected increase of inflation.

101. (C) GDP includes any final production that occurs within the country mentioned. Therefore, the production of the restaurant would be counted in England's GDP, and NOT in the GDP of the United States.

102. (E) Choice (E) is correct. The labor force is employed workers plus unemployed workers. Since Jessica has recently graduated from college but has not yet taken the job at IBM, this would leave the labor force unchanged.

103. (E) Choice (E) is correct. People who are not actively looking for work are not considered part of the labor force.

104. (A) Choice (A) is the best answer because hyperinflation describes an extremely rapid increase in the price level. A gradual increase of the price level over time would not be considered hyperinflation. Choice (C) is not the correct answer because the value of money falls during hyperinflation.

105. (E) Choice (E) is correct. Remember the formula for calculating GDP: C + I + G + (X − M). You must plug in the numbers and find what is missing to answer this question, where C = $4 million, I = $2 million, G = $5 million, and X is $4 million: 4 + 2 + 5 + (4 − ?) = $15 million.

106. (A) Choice (A) is the best answer because marshmallows used in ice cream would be considered an intermediate good. Choices (B), (C), (D), and (E) are all considered final goods.

107. (B) Choice (B) is the best answer because establishing a price index helps economists, businesses, and the government compare prices over time. Establishing a rate of inflation and nominal prices versus real prices would not be necessary without a base year of comparison. Choice (A) is incorrect because it refers to the GDP price deflator. Choice (C) is incorrect because it refers to inflation. Choice (D) is incorrect because it refers to the peak of a business cycle.

108. (D) The underground economy refers to both illegal activities and economic activities unreported. Choice (D) is the best answer because the sale of a used car at a car dealership is neither illegal nor unreported.

109. (C) Choice (C) is correct. Nominal GDP refers to the current value of output using current prices. It is different from real GDP because real GDP measures the value of current output compared to prices at a fixed point in time.

110. (B) Choice (B) is correct. Businesses purchase the factors of production from households in the resource market.

111. (D) In the circular flow model, the government taxes and spends in the product market and the factor market, with firms and households. They do not interact in the expanded circular flow model which includes exports or imports.

112. (D) Choice (D) is correct. The television set is a finished good.

113. (C) Choice (C) is correct. Used goods aren't included in GDP.

114. (B) Choice (B) is correct. GDP does not include income earned abroad.

115. (A) Choice (A) is correct. Businesses purchase resources and consumers purchase goods.

116. (A) Choice (A) is correct. Government spending is included in the GDP, so the increase in government spending would increase GDP proportionally.

117. (C) Choice (C) is correct. Net imports are a component of GDP.

118. (E) The correct sequence to follow in a traditional business cycle is: expansion, peak, contraction, trough, recovery.

119. (B) Choice (B) is correct. Government spending and investment increase the consumption of goods and services.

120. (A) When products are imported from foreign countries, payments flow out of the country to the foreign nation. Those payments are called leakages from the circular flow model.

121. (B) Choice (B) is correct. GDP = C (2,000) + I (500) + G (1,000) + (X – M) (100 – 200) = $3,400.

122. (A) Choice (A) is correct. Consumer purchasing power would double.

123. (C) Choice (C) is the best answer. The price of a select basket of goods would increase by 300 percent.

124. (A) Choice (A) is correct. If the price index is more than 100, real GDP is less than nominal GDP.

125. (A) Choice (A) is correct. Bob does not have the skill set that employers currently demand, so he is structurally unemployed.

126. (A) Choice (A) is the best answer. Structural unemployment occurs because unemployed workers don't have the right skills for available jobs, so job training programs would be the most effective way to fix the problem.

127. (B) When labor is employed, the employees have done any work at all for pay or profit during the survey reference week. Therefore, part-time employees are considered employed.

128. (B) Choice (B) is correct. When a worker leaves a job to search for another job, this is considered frictional unemployment.

129. (D) Choice (D) is correct. The labor force includes unemployed workers, but does not include people who are not searching for work.

130. (C) Choice (C) is correct. The workforce is 300 – 20 = 280 million people. The number of unemployed workers would be 280 – 250 = 30 million people.

131. (B) Choice (B) is correct. The number of employed workers is 100 – 10 – 20 = 70 million.

132. (C) Choice (C) is correct. United Television sold 100 television sets and 50 of them came from inventory, so it must have produced 50 television sets, which are worth $100 each, adding $5,000 to GDP.

133. (D) Choice (D) is correct. Inventory increased by 80 – 50 = 30 cars. The firm sold 60 cars, so output was 30 + 60 = 90 cars. The cars sell for $10,000 each, so the contribution to GDP is $900,000.

134. (B) Choice (B) is correct. A negative inflation rate is known as deflation.

135. (A) Choice (A) is correct. A decrease in the inflation rate is known as disinflation.

136. (C) The calculation for GDP is C + I + G + (X – M). So, to calculate this, GDP would be $100 + $75 + $250 + ($50 – $75) = $400. Taxes are not included in the calculation for GDP.

137. (A) Choice (A) is correct. The recession caused the factory workers to lose their jobs so they are cyclically unemployed.

138. (E) Choice (E) is correct. If students aren't searching for work, they are not considered part of the labor force.

139. (D) Choice (D) is correct. The company sold 300 refrigerators, and 50 of them came from inventory, so output was 250 refrigerators. At a price of $400 each, this is $100,000 added to GDP.

140. (A) Choice (A) is correct. The company sold 250 ovens and added 100 ovens to inventory, so output was 350 ovens. The ovens are worth $100 each, so $35,000 was added to GDP.

141. (C) Choice (C) is correct. Sally must add the real interest rate, 10 percent, plus the inflation rate, –2 percent, to get the required return, 8 percent.

142. (E) Choice (E) is correct. Because Joe is not currently looking for work, he is not considered to be unemployed.

143. (D) Choice (D) is correct. Deflation is a decrease in the price level.

144. (D) The calculation for the real rate interest is equal to the nominal interest rate minus the rate of inflation. In this case, the formula would be equal to 5% – 3% = 2%.

145. (E) Frictional unemployment is defined as unemployment as a result of searching for a new or different job. A student searching for a job upon completion of her schooling is considered frictionally unemployed.

146. (C) Choice (C) is correct. The formula for GDP is C + I + G + (X – M). Plugging in the numbers results in the formula ? + 5 + 4 + (3 – 6) = 20. For the equation to balance, consumer spending must be $14 million.

147. (A) Choice (A) is correct. The formula for GDP is C + I + G + (X – M). Plugging in the numbers results in the formula 8 + 6 + 10 + (5 – ?) = 25. For the equation to balance, imports must be $4 million.

148. (D) Choice (D) is correct. The sheet metal is an intermediate good, not a final product.

149. (D) Choice (D) is correct. The underground economy includes unreported transactions and illegal activities.

150. (B) Choice (B) is correct. Dividing the current value by the base index value results in a percentage, such as 110 percent, that provides the value of the price index.

151. (A) The substitution bias of consumers occurs when the current prices of goods within the market basket increase and consumers purchase other goods that may not be in the market basket. That value of change in consumer behavior is not included in the consumer price index.

152. (B) Choice (B) is correct. The price increased by 50 percent so the price index is 150.

153. (C) Choice (C) is correct. The price fell 20 percent so the new price index is 80.

154. (B) Choice (B) is correct. The workforce is 500 – 40 = 460 million people. The number of unemployed workers would be 460 – 400 = 60 million people.

155. (C) Choice (C) is correct. The number of employed workers is 240 – 30 – 20 = 190.

156. (B) Choice (B) is correct. The crab fishing boat only needs workers for part of the year, so the fishing workers are seasonally unemployed.

157. (B) Choice (B) is correct. The formula for GDP is C + I + G + (X – M). Plugging in the numbers results in the formula 10 + 7 + 15 + (? – 11) = 30. For the equation to balance, exports must be $9 million.

158. (C) Choice (C) is correct. The price index for 1995 is 100 × (240/200), or 120.

159. (C) Choice (C) is correct. The first two choices are production inputs.

160. (C) Choice (C) is correct. A decrease of 25 percent in the price index would increase purchasing power by 50 percent.

161. (D) Choice (D) is the best answer. The price of a select basket of goods would increase by 50 percent.

162. (B) Choice (B) is correct. The labor force only includes workers who are employed or searching for work.

163. (B) Choice (B) is correct. The labor force is (180 – 10) = 170 million and (170 – 120) = 50 million unemployed workers.

164. (B) Choice (B) is correct. Rocky Mountain Sports sold 300 tents and 100 of them came from inventory, so output was 200 tents. The tents were worth $50 each, so output was $10,000.

165. (C) According to their loan contracts, borrowers who have loans that are calculated at a fixed rate do not have to pay the increase in inflationary costs associated with an unexpected increase in the rate of inflation.

166. (D) All of the options offered are included in the calculation for the United States GDP except the purchasing of sugar by the cookie manufacturer. The new car, although from a Japanese company, is made domestically. The new home is considered investment. The frosting is consumption. The aircraft carrier is government spending. The sugar would be considered an intermediate good and therefore only counted when the finished cookies have been purchased.

167. (A) Choice (A) is correct. Real income increased by less than nominal income because of inflation.

168. (B) Choice (B) is correct. An increase from $10 to $12 is a 20 percent increase, but inflation was 5 percent so the real increase is 15 percent.

169. (E) When the government and central bank actively work toward decreasing the rate of inflation, it is called disinflation. Deflation is defined as a general decrease of the rate of inflation below zero or into the negative.

170. (A) Stagflation is defined as the combination of inflation and stagnating or falling aggregate output, causing increased unemployment.

Chapter 3: National Income and Price Determination

171. (B) Choice (B) is correct. The aggregate demand curve follows the law of demand: quantity demanded decreases as price increases.

172. (A) Choice (A) is correct. Full employment is the absence of structural unemployment.

173. (C) Choice (C) is correct. The multiplier effect explains any change in spending, such as consumer consumption, investment, or government spending, that has a greater effect on actual output.

174. (B) Choice (B) is the best answer because a change in price level will reflect only a change in the quantity demanded and not an actual shift of the aggregate demand curve. Choices (A), (C), (D), and (E) are all determinants of aggregate demand that could shift the curve to the left or right.

175. (A) A rightward shift of the aggregate supply curve represents economic growth. Choice (A) is the best answer because an increase in productivity increases output and would shift the curve to the right. Choice (B) is incorrect because that would increase costs for producers and therefore shift the curve to the left. Choice (C) is incorrect because increased government regulations would restrict output and cause a leftward shift of the curve. Choice (D) is incorrect because that would shift only the aggregate demand curve to the right.

176. (B) Choice (B) is correct. This is the definition of an aggregate supply curve. According to the law of supply, producers are willing and able to produce more at higher price levels, and vice versa. This reflects a direct relationship between price and output.

177. (B) Choice (B) is correct. A leftward shift of the aggregate supply curve shows a decrease in economic output. If workers' wages decreased, a major cost to producers would decrease. This would push the aggregate supply curve to the right.

178. (B) Choice (B) is correct. An increase in the price level will increase the demand for money.

179. (A) Choice (A) is correct. The multiplier effect explains any change in spending, such as consumer consumption, investment, or government spending, that has a greater effect on actual output. The multiplier effect is not strongly felt if the price level rises and weakens the impact of increased spending.

180. (E) Choice (E) is correct. You must use the formula $1/(1 - MPC)$, or $1/0.2 = 5$. Then $5 \times \$10$ billion = an increase of $50 billion.

181. (C) Choice (C) is the best answer because if supply decreases while demand for a good or service increases, an increase in the price level will result.

182. (A) Labor costs are a determinant of aggregate supply. Increasing labor costs would cause the aggregate supply curve to decrease or shift to the left.

183. (B) Choice (B) is correct. The long-run aggregate supply curve is vertical in the long run. The long run represents enough time for producers to make adjustments to production and workers' wages to adjust to real wages.

184. (C) Choice (C) is correct. Stagflation exists when inflation and unemployment increase at the same time. Choice (C) is the best answer because supply shock is a drastic and rapid change to the determinants of aggregate supply. If an event occurs, such as cost-push inflation or a new government regulation, this may affect aggregate supply, thus affecting the inflation rate and unemployment rate.

185. (C) Choice (C) is correct because equilibrium will always refer to the point where total output demanded equals total output supplied. Choice (A) is incorrect because it refers to the recessionary gap. Choice (B) is incorrect because it refers to the inflationary gap. Choice (D) is incorrect because it refers to deflation. Choice (E) is incorrect because it refers to a recession.

186. (A) Choice (A) is the best answer because an increase in government spending will show an increase in the calculation of GDP: G = government spending in $C + I + G + (X - M)$. All other choices reflect a decrease in specific parts of the economy.

187. (B) Choice (B) is the correct answer because a recessionary gap refers to the amount by which full-employment GDP exceeds the equilibrium of real GDP. Choice (A) is incorrect because an inflationary gap refers to the amount by which equilibrium at real GDP exceeds full employment. Choice (C) is incorrect because it refers to a rapid and drastic increase in the price level. Choice (D) is incorrect because it refers to when inflation and unemployment increase at the same time. Choice (E) is incorrect because it refers to the GDP falling for six consecutive months.

188. (A) Choice (A) is correct. The Phillips curve illustrates the inverse relationship between unemployment and inflation. The lower the unemployment, the higher the rate of inflation, and vice versa. Just like the aggregate supply curve in the long run, the Phillips curve is vertical in the long run.

189. (C) Choice (C) is correct. The Phillips curve illustrates the inverse relationship between unemployment and inflation. The lower the unemployment, the higher the rate of inflation, and vice versa.

190. (D) Choice (D) is correct. The multiplier effect explains any change in spending—such as consumer consumption, investment, or government spending—that has a greater effect on actual output.

191. (A) Choice (A) is correct. The crowding out effect involves government borrowing to fund government spending. The choices that do not refer to the government may be disregarded. When the government increases its borrowing, it essentially crowds out private investment. Therefore, the real connection is between government borrowing/spending and private investment and consumption.

192. (C) The answer to this question involves a rightward shift of the aggregate demand curve, so you are looking for actions that would increase the GDP. Choice (C) is the best answer because an increase in government spending will result in an increase in the GDP. All other choices involve contracting the GDP.

193. (A) A supply shock is an event or action that rapidly increases or decreases total output, shifting the aggregate supply curve to the left or right. Choice (A) is the best answer because discovery of new resources would increase the amount of total output very quickly. Choices (B), (C), and (D) would occur over a longer period of time.

194. (A) Choice (A) is correct. The multiplier effect explains any change in spending—such as consumer consumption, investment, or government spending—that has a greater effect on actual output. The question asks for the effect of an increase in government spending, which would increase the GDP; so any answer that results in a decrease should be eliminated.

195. (A) Choice (A) is correct. The long-run aggregate supply (LRAS) curve is vertical because enough time has passed for total output to adjust to the price level. At this point, it is assumed that the LRAS is independent of changes in price, and output is determined by other factors of production.

196. (A) Choice (A) is correct. Gross domestic product (GDP) is an excellent measure of the health of a nation's economy by measuring the total amount of income generated in a country for a year. Choices (B), (C), and (D) are irrelevant when questioning what the GDP indicates.

197. (D) Choice (D) is correct. Supply-side economists support stimulating aggregate supply by promoting policies that encourage investment and entrepreneurship. Such policies would enact tax breaks that would increase disposable incomes, and hopefully increase household savings and investments in businesses. Choice (A) is incorrect because that money could be used as tax breaks for individuals. Choice (B) is incorrect because that would stimulate aggregate demand, not supply. Choice (C) is incorrect because a decrease in government spending and investment often leads to increased unemployment.

198. (B) One of the main tactics used to battle the Great Depression was an increase in government spending. Increasing government spending would increase the GDP and result in a shift of the aggregate demand curve to the right. Therefore, any answer with a decrease in government spending should be eliminated. If there is an increase in taxes, there would be less consumer consumption because people would have less disposable income. Choice (B) is the best answer.

199. (B) When production costs, especially nominal wages, are fixed in the short run, the aggregate supply curve has a positive or upward-sloping shape.

200. (C) The long-run aggregate supply curve illustrates the relationship between the aggregate price level and GDP if all prices including input costs were fully flexible. It occurs vertically at the full employment level of GDP.

201. (C) Choice (C) is correct. Consumers who receive pension income will have a higher MPC.

202. (A) Choice (A) is correct. Consumers with higher MPC are more likely to shop at locally owned businesses.

203. (D) Choice (D) is correct. An increase in imports does not result in a higher GDP.

204. (C) Choice (C) is correct. Tax cuts don't provide as much of a multiplier effect as other stimulus measures.

205. (E) Choice (E) is correct. A decrease in imports would shift the aggregate demand curve to the right because net exports would increase.

206. (B) Choice (B) is correct. An increase in worker wages would result in higher production costs and shift the aggregate supply curve to the left.

207. (D) In the long run, if the government takes no action to correct a recession due to the higher-than-natural rate of unemployment, labor will accept lower wages. This decrease in the costs of production will cause the short-run aggregate supply curve to move right, correcting the recessionary gap and decreasing unemployment.

208. (C) Choice (C) is correct. The interest rate effect explains why an increase in the price level will result in higher interest rates.

209. (B) Choice (B) is correct. Imports would decrease and exports would increase because domestic products would be less expensive.

210. (E) The increase of the overall price level (inflation) in the United States would make goods from the United States more expensive, causing less foreign purchases of U.S. goods and therefore a decline in exports from the United States.

211. (A) Choice (A) is correct. An increase in the price level weakens, but does not eliminate, the multiplier effect.

212. (C) Choice (C) is correct. This situation would be considered deflation.

213. (B) Choice (B) is correct. This situation would be an inflationary gap.

214. (A) Choice (A) is correct. A contractionary fiscal policy aims to decrease inflation by decreasing aggregate demand and supply. Increasing taxes will decrease consumption, while decreasing government spending, as part of the formula for the GDP, will shift the aggregate supply curve to the left.

215. (B) Choice (B) is the best answer because this is a contractionary fiscal policy. When the government implements a contractionary fiscal policy, it is usually trying to deal with high prices brought on by inflation.

216. (D) Choice (D) is the best answer because falling demand and rising supply will result in a lower price level.

217. (C) Choice (C) is correct. If the price of a necessity good rises, and substitute goods are not available, firms must raise prices for their output and the price level will rise.

218. (B) Choice (B) is correct. A positive shock to aggregate supply will result in a lower price level, as well as higher output.

219. (C) Choice (C) is correct. This situation is known as macroeconomic equilibrium.

220. (C) In the long run, if the government takes no action to correct rising inflation, labor will need higher wages to offset the rising inflation. This increase in the costs of production will cause the short-run aggregate supply curve to move left, correcting the inflationary gap and increasing unemployment.

221. (C) The downward-sloping curve on the graph displays the negative relationship between the price level and the level of real GDP. This is more commonly referred to as the aggregate demand curve.

222. (D) The current state of the economy in this graph is shown as the intersection of curves A and C. At this point, the level of real GDP is higher than the long-run full employment level and therefore places the current state of the economy in a recessionary gap.

223. (E) The full employment level of real GDP occurs at the point where the long-run aggregate supply curve intersects with the horizontal access. This point represents the level of real GDP that is equivalent to its potential output.

224. (E) Any increase in the determinants of aggregate demand (C + I + G + Xn) will cause a shift of AD to the right. Consumption increasing will cause GDP to rise as shown by aggregate demand shifting to the right.

225. (C) As aggregate demand shifts left along the short-run aggregate supply, the general price level (inflation) will decrease and GDP will decrease, causing the level of unemployment to increase.

226. (E) Choice (E) is correct. This chart shows the classical section of the AD–AS graph. Increases in demand won't increase output or employment any further.

227. (C) Choice (C) is correct. Aggregate supply is vertical when the economy is at full employment and maximum output because neither variable can increase further.

228. (B) Choice (B) is the best answer. Keynesian policies can make output move along the aggregate supply curve by reducing unemployment or increasing consumption, but shifting the curve requires an increase in the economy's production capacity. This could be done through infrastructure investments.

229. (C) Choice (C) is the best answer. Higher raw material prices reduce aggregate supply.

230. (A) Choice (A) is correct. This situation will result in an inflationary gap.

Chapter 4: The Financial Sector

231. (B) Choice (B) is correct. Money is an effective medium of exchange because it is always accepted as payment, while a merchant might not accept other goods or services in trade.

232. (B) Choice (B) is correct. M1 money refers to all coins and paper currency and all money in checking accounts (checkable deposits). This is the most readily available form of money. Choices (A), (C), and (D) are part of M2 money.

233. (D) Choice (D) is correct. A bond represents a debt from the issuer to the person to whom the bond is made. People buy U.S. bonds, and the government promises to pay back that money plus interest after a certain period of time.

234. (C) The M1 measure of the money supply is defined as currency in circulation, traveler's checks, and checkable deposits.

235. (C) The M2 measure of the money supply is defined as everything that is a part of M1, certificates of deposit, savings accounts, and money market mutual funds. Therefore, as currency held by consumers is a part of M1, it is also a part of M2.

236. (B) Choice (B) is the best answer because checkable deposits are part of the M1 money supply: money that is the most liquid and easily accessible. Therefore, M1 would increase and M2 would remain the same.

237. (C) Choice (C) is correct. The money used in the United States is backed and supported by the U.S. government. The United States does not have a gold standard anymore as in Choice (D), nor is it backed by valuable land as in Choice (B). Money has value because the U.S. government decrees it does.

238 (A) Choice (A) is correct. The long-run aggregate supply curve is vertical in the long run. The long run represents enough time for producers to make adjustments to production and workers' wages to adjust to real wages. All other choices will have an effect on real GDP.

239. (B) Choice (B) is correct. There is an inverse relationship between the price of bonds and the established interest rate. This is so because if you bought a bond for $100 with a 5 percent interest rate and the interest rate drops to 4 percent over the next few years, then you lost a 1 percent value on that bond.

240. (A) Choice (A) is correct. The Federal Open Market Committee (FOMC) is part of the Federal Reserve System where a board of governors meets to decide monetary policy. They decide to either increase or decrease the money supply by buying/selling government securities or raising/lowering interest rates.

241. (A) Choice (A) is correct. Higher interest rates would discourage the use of credit.

242. (A) The Federal Reserve System utilizes monetary policy to control the money supply and stimulate the economy. In order to decrease or increase the money supply, a main tool of the Fed is to buy and sell government securities from commercial banks. Choices (B), (C), (D), and (E) are all functions of the Fed, but Choice (A) is the most significant.

243. (E) Choice (E) is correct. M1 money refers to all coins and paper currency and all money in checking accounts (checkable deposits). The most significant characteristic of M1 money is that it is held by the public. Institutions like the federal government and the Fed would not be a part of M1 money supply.

244. (D) The money creation process is mainly controlled by banks through their ability to loan to businesses and consumers. This does not print more money, but simply allows more people to access the available currency in circulation, creating more spending and saving.

245. (B) Choice (B) is correct. If interest rates increase, more money is required to pay back loans, from mortgage payments on a house to everyday purchases with a credit card. This would constrict the money supply, and the demand for money would decrease.

246. (A) Open market operations are one of three tools available to the central bank with which it can influence the economy by buying and selling treasury securities in the bond market. This process makes more or less currency available in the money market, which influences interest rates and, as a result, also rates of investment. They can also change the required reserve ratio (RRR) and increase or decrease the discount rate.

247. (C) A bank's total reserves are the actual amount the bank has on hand in its vaults and any money on reserve at the Fed. Choice (C) is the best answer because it calculates the bank's cash and money on reserve at the Fed. All other choices are miscalculations.

248. (A) Choice (A) is correct. Remember that money is created through debt. If a loan is made to an individual for $5,000, then the bank created that amount of money into the money supply. Leo's initial deposit would only increase the M1 money supply.

249. (B) The central bank requires commercial banks to "reserve" a percentage of their checkable deposits. The bank is then allowed to lend out the remainder in order to create profits for the bank through interest on those loans, as well as helping currency to circulate through the economy. This process is called fractional reserve banking.

250. (C) A major problem of banks that led to the Great Depression was the lack of monitoring and influence by the government. Requiring banks to have a percentage of their money on reserve is a method of controlling and influencing the banks. Choice (C) is the best answer.

251. (A) Choice (A) is correct. One of the main and most significant goals of monetary policy instituted by the Federal Reserve Bank is to help the economy grow or contract based on the current state of the economy. The economy goes through a business cycle:

expansion, peak, contraction, trough, and recovery. Varying the money supply (to help the economy grow or contract) is a valuable tool of the Federal Reserve.

252. (C) Choice (C) is correct. M1 money refers to all coins and paper currency and all money in checking accounts (checkable deposits).

253. (A) Choice (A) is correct. M2 money is M1 money plus savings, time-related deposits, and noninstitutional money market funds.

254. (A) Choice (A) is correct. The money from S1 to S2 represents a decrease in the money supply. Any answer that references an increase should be eliminated. When the money supply decreases, the Fed is instituting a tight money policy, which would contract the economy. One significant way to implement this is for the Fed to purchase government securities.

255. (C) Choice (C) is the best answer because usually the Fed institutes a contraction-ary monetary policy as a way to battle inflation. If prices are too high, then the money supply is too high; therefore, the Fed should reduce the money supply to combat inflation.

256. (D) Choice (D) is correct. Transactions demand and asset demand comprise the two components for the demand for money. Transactions demand is money kept for purchases and has a direct relationship with the GDP; asset demand is money kept for a store of value for later use and is inversely related with the GDP.

257. (A) Choice (A) is correct. A stock is a certified piece of paper that represents a claim of ownership in a business.

258. (A) Choice (A) is correct. A bond represents a debt from the issuer to the person to whom the bond is made. People buy U.S. bonds, and the government promises to pay back that money plus interest after a certain period of time.

259. (B) Choice (B) is correct. The Federal Reserve Bank is responsible for maintaining the money supply for the United States. The federal government controls fiscal policy, which involves taxes and government spending and borrowing.

260. (A) To calculate the money multiplier: 1/RR or 1/0.1 = 10. Then 10 × $500 = $5,000. You must then subtract Jack's original $500, as it was already in circulation and was not part of the new money created. Therefore, $5,000 − $500 = $4,500 in new money created.

261. (B) Choice (B) is the best answer because a unit of account is money being used as a standard of measurement for the value and/or cost of goods and services.

262. (E) Choice (E) is the best answer because a medium of exchange is an intermediary used in the exchange of goods and services, such as paper money.

263. (C) The Federal Reserve System is responsible for implementing monetary policy. Choices (A), (B), (D), and (E) are all facets of monetary policy, whereas Choice (C) refers to tax rates, which is part of fiscal policy and is implemented by the federal government.

264. (C) Choice (C) is the best answer because demand deposits are a liability of the bank, not an asset. An asset of the bank is anything owned by the bank. Choices (A), (B), (D), and (E) are assets that belong to a bank.

265. (B) When currency/money is being used to set prices and make economic calculations, it is being used as a unit of account.

266. (C) Choice (C) is correct. The central bank of the United States is the Federal Reserve Bank. It is responsible for regulating monetary policy and the financial system.

267. (A) Choice (A) is correct. M1 money refers to all coins and paper currency and all money in checking accounts (checkable deposits). Traveler's checks are often used as cash by people on vacation and would therefore be part of the M1 money supply.

268. (A) Choice (A) is the best answer because it correctly calculates the money multiplier, $1/0.05 = 20$.

269. (C) Choice (C) is the best answer because increasing the reserve ratio will decrease the money supply. If banks are required to increase the amount of cash they must keep in their vaults, then that decreases the lending power of the bank. If banks are making fewer loans to businesses and individuals, then the money supply will decrease.

270. (A) Choice (A) is correct. Remember that there is an inverse relationship between the price of a bond and inflation.

271. (E) Choice (E) is the best answer because a bank's biggest liability is checkable deposits. The banks are responsible for being able to provide and account for that money on hand. Remember that checkable deposits are part of M1 money, which is the most liquid and available form of money in an economy.

272. (A) Choice (A) is correct. Remember that there is an inverse relationship between the price of a bond and inflation.

273. (B) While all answer choices are items banks would consider assets, the loans made to customers are the largest segment. The bank expects repayment, which is why they are assets, and almost all banks loan out more than the cash they receive from their customers.

274. (C) Choice (C) is correct. Money is an effective measure of value because it is easier to set a price for goods using money than it is to set a price using other trade goods.

275. (D) Choice (D) is correct. A dollar bill would be the most liquid store of value.

276. (A) Choice (A) is correct. Traveler's checks are considered cash so they are part of the M1 money supply.

277. (C) Choice (C) is the best answer. A bond is a store of value that provides investment income in exchange for investment risk. Cash doesn't provide any protection from inflation. The consumer does give up liquidity by purchasing a bond because the bond has to be sold for cash before its value can be used to purchase goods and services, or held until all of the interest is collected.

278. (E) Choice (E) is correct. Because the bank took possession of the roll of quarters, the supply of currency available to consumers, which is part of M1, has decreased. Meanwhile, the amount of money in savings accounts, which is part of M2, has increased by the same amount, and since M2 includes M1, the quarters are still in M2.

279. (B) Choice (B) is correct. The store traded the cash for a checkable deposit, and both of these are included in M1. Neither M1 nor M2 will change as a result of the transaction.

280. (D) Choice (D) is correct. If prices fall by 75 percent, an item that costs $1 now only costs $0.25. This means the dollar gained 400 percent in purchasing power.

281. (B) Choice (B) is correct. A decrease in the money supply or an increase in the demand for money would result in higher interest rates.

282. (C) The nominal interest rate is determined within the money market. When the money supply increases, it moves along a downward-sloping money demand curve, causing the nominal interest rate to decline.

283. (B) Choice (B) is correct. Lower interest rates would encourage the use of credit.

284. (D) The process of lending, borrowing, and redepositing is called money creation. When a bank lends to a borrower, it is making some of its excess reserves from demand deposits available to be used in the economy. This increases the money supply within the economy through the multiplier process.

285. (C) Choice (C) is correct. The bank's reserves are its cash and Federal Reserve deposits, which add up to $10 million. It has to keep 20 percent of the value of its reserves but can lend out the other 80 percent, or $8 million.

286. (C) Choice (C) is correct. The bank made loans worth 90 percent of its assets. If the loans are worth $18 million, its assets are worth $20 million. If $10 million is at the Fed, cash on hand must be $10 million.

287. (B) Choice (B) is correct. If interest rates decrease, less money would be needed to pay back loans. The money supply would increase, and the demand for money would increase.

288. (B) Choice (B) is correct. The loan repayment would reduce the supply of money by $4,000 and the checking account deposit would have no effect.

289. (D) Choice (D) is correct. When the bank makes a loan, its assets increase and its liabilities show no change.

290. (D) Choice (D) is correct. The first bank can loan out $1,600, and if this cash is deposited at another bank, the second bank can loan out $1,280, and so on. If this process continues, the amount of money created is excess reserves times (1 divided by the reserve ratio) or $2,000 × 1/(0.20), which is $10,000.

291. (B) Choice (B) is correct. The same process works in reverse. The amount of money removed from the money supply would be $4,000 × (1/0.25), which is $16,000.

292. (C) Choice (C) is correct. The Federal Reserve can increase the supply of money by reducing the reserve requirement for commercial banks, or it can reduce the discount rate.

293. (C) Choice (C) is correct. The Federal Reserve can reduce the supply of money by raising the reserve requirement or increasing the discount rate.

294. (B) Choice (B) is correct. The bank loaned out 80 percent of its reserves, which is $32 million. The remaining 20 percent of its reserves must be worth $8 million, for a total of $40 million. If the bank has $20 million in cash on hand, it must have another $20 million at the Federal Reserve for its total reserves to equal $40 million.

295. (B) This is also equivalent to the value of the bond purchase times the money multiplier. If the reserve ratio is 20 percent: $1,000 bond purchase/0.20 = $5,000, just as the money multiplier is 1/RR or 1/0.20 = 5, multiplied by the bond purchase: $1,000 × 5 = $5,000.

296. (E) When money is held by banks or borrowers as currency rather than redeposited or loaned out, it causes the multiplier effect to be decreased, as the money does not freely circulate to be multiplied by future banks. Therefore, the only way that the maximum amount of money creation can take place is if banks loan out all of their excess reserves and borrowers redeposit all of their borrowed funds.

297. (B) Choice (B) is correct. The Federal Reserve can buy government securities to increase the money supply, in addition to reducing the discount rate or reducing the reserve requirement.

298. (B) Choice (B) is correct. A shift in the money supply to the right is an increase in the money supply, which could be produced by the Federal Reserve buying government securities on the open market.

299. (E) Choice (E) is the best answer. Increasing the money supply is one way to stimulate the economy out of a recession.

300. (A) Choice (A) is the best answer because selling government securities would decrease the money supply and as a result decrease inflation. Choices (D) and (E) are incorrect because income taxes are included only in fiscal policy.

301. (C) An expansionary monetary policy aims to increase the money supply and increase aggregate demand. As a result, employment will increase. Choice (C) is the best answer.

302. (A) Choice (A) is correct. You must use the money multiplier to answer this question. 1/(1 − MPC) or 1/(1 − 0.7) = 1/0.3 = 3.33. Then 3.33 × 10 = 33 billion.

303. (B) Choice (B) is correct. Money is being used as a unit of account for the hamburger.

304. (A) Choice (A) is correct. The hamburger restaurant deposited the money in the bank as a store of value.

305. (C) The price of previously issued bonds and interest rates are inverse, or move in opposite directions. Therefore, if interest rates are falling due to the securities purchase, bond prices will rise.

306. (D) The buying and selling of securities on the open market is called open market operations. When the central bank engages in open market operations to combat a recession, it will buy securities to increase the money supply and decrease the interest rate.

307. (E) A rising price level will cause more consumers within the economy to keep cash or currency on hand in order to buy the things that they need.

308. (A) In the money market, a downward-sloping curve represents the relationship between the two axes. Those are the nominal interest rate and the quantity of money.

309. (D) Choice (D) is the best answer. If the money supply shifts to the right, the interest rate falls.

310. (A) Choice (A) is correct. The Federal Reserve decides whether the money supply shifts to the left or the right. Other organizations can only change the demand for money.

311. (C) Choice (C) is correct. The bank has reserves worth $40 million (cash plus Federal Reserve deposits). It must keep 5 percent of this, which is $2 million. It can lend out the other $38 million.

312. (C) Choice (C) is the best answer. The interest rate would fall from 6 percent to 4 percent.

313. (E) Choice (E) is the best answer. A money supply of $50 billion would result in a 6 percent interest rate, so if the interest rate is higher than that, the money supply must be lower.

314. (E) Choice (E) is correct. The interest rate would change from 6 percent to less than 3 percent.

315. (B) Choice (B) is correct. On the DM3 curve, the interest rate is 9 percent when the money supply is $20 billion.

Chapter 5: Long-Run Consequences of Stabilization Policies

316. (D) The government can implement fiscal policy through taxes and spending.

317. (C) Choice (C) is correct. The original Phillips curve could not explain stagflation.

318. (B) Choice (B) is correct. The Phillips curve predicts that inflation will fall if unemployment rises.

319. (C) Choice (C) is the best answer because discretionary fiscal policy refers to actions taken by the federal government that do not happen automatically. Choice (A) is irrelevant to this question. Choice (B) would be the exact opposite of what the government hopes to achieve. Choice (D) is incorrect because nondiscretionary fiscal policy refers to changes in government expenditures that happen automatically without government implementation. Choice (E) is incorrect because monetary policy is regulated by the Fed.

320. (A) Choice (A) is correct. A decrease in aggregate demand is represented by a leftward shift of the aggregate demand curve. This would result from a tight, or contractionary, fiscal policy.

321. (C) Choice (C) is correct. Remember that when the government implements a tax, it serves as a transfer of money from the people to the government; when the government increases government spending, it serves as a transfer of money from the government to the people. Having both a decrease in taxes and a decrease in government spending would, therefore, counteract each other.

322. (A) Choice (A) is correct. Demand-pull inflation refers to inflation caused by an increasing aggregate demand (AD) as it moves toward the upward sloping range of aggregate supply. Therefore, the goal is to move the AD curve from AD3 to AD2, which necessitates a contractionary fiscal policy. Choice (A) is the best answer because increasing taxes would decrease purchasing power of consumers and thus decrease aggregate demand.

323. (D) Because you are looking for an increase in real GDP, you may disregard any answer that suggests a decrease in government spending. This would result in a rightward shift of the AD curve, and the only viable option is Choice (D).

324. (B) If the country is in a recession, then the government wants to stimulate the economy by increasing the GDP. This requires an increase to one of the determinants of calculating the GDP: consumer spending, investment, government spending, and the difference between exports and imports. Therefore, you may disregard any answer that elects to decrease government spending. Choices (A) and (D) are incorrect because these two policies would counteract each other. Choice (B) is the best answer.

325. (A) Choice (A) is correct. This is another multiplier question, and the formula is $1/(1 - MPC)$, but remember that the question gave the marginal propensity to save ($MPS = 0.4$), so this must be subtracted from 1 to get the marginal propensity to consume ($MPC = 0.6$). $1/(1 - 0.6) = 1/(0.4) = 2.5$. $2.5x = 50$ billion. If the government wished to increase the aggregate demand by $50 billion, then it should increase government spending by $20 billion.

326. (D) Choice (D) is correct. A built-in stabilizer will act automatically without specific policy actions of the government. Transfer payments refer to payments made by the government for social welfare programs. If income increases, then transfer payments tend to decrease.

327. (E) Choice (E) is the best answer because if the economy is at full employment, disposable income will increase and result in inflation due to the increase in consumers' purchasing power.

328. (A) Choice (A) is correct. The crowding out effect involves government borrowing to fund government spending.

329. (B) Choices (C) and (D) refer to monetary policy, which is regulated by the Fed, so these answers may be eliminated because the question refers to fiscal policy. Choice (B) is the best answer because an expansionary policy will increase aggregate demand. As a result, the dollar will appreciate and make goods and services more expensive to foreigners. Therefore, net exports will tend to fall with an expansionary policy.

330. (A) Choice (A) is correct. A progressive tax system refers to how the proportion of taxes paid increases with an increase in income. This is the only acceptable answer out of the choices.

331. (A) Choice (A) is the best answer because government spending has a larger impact on aggregate demand than taxes.

332. (D) Choice (D) is correct. Demand-pull inflation refers to inflation caused by an increasing aggregate demand as it moves toward the upward sloping range of aggregate supply. If there is an increase in the money supply, an increase in aggregate demand will result.

333. (C) Choice (C) is correct. Cost-push inflation refers to an increase in price level due to an increase in the costs of production. Cost-push inflation will occur if no gains in productivity are seen.

334. (A) Choice (A) is correct. Just like the LRAS curve, the Phillips curve will be vertical in the long run. The Phillips curve measures the inverse relationship between inflation and unemployment. With economic growth, inflation increases, which should lead to an increase in employment.

335. (A) Choice (A) is correct. The consumer price index (CPI) measures changes in the price level of consumer goods and services. Therefore, the purchasing power of the dollar is also measured through the CPI. If prices increase by 33 percent, this corresponds to a 25 percent decline in the purchasing power of the dollar.

336. (D) Choice (D) is correct. If GDP falls for two consecutive quarters, then the society is in an official recession.

337. (E) Choice (E) is correct. The quantity theory of money states that as the money supply increases, higher prices will result and not affect real output. Choice (A) is incorrect because it describes the money multiplier. Choice (B) is incorrect because it refers to the federal funds rate. Choice (C) is incorrect because it refers to half of the equation to calculate the exchange rate. Choice (D) is incorrect because it refers to the velocity of money.

338. (A) The idea behind monetization is the action of the Federal Reserve to buy government securities and increase the money supply. Any increase in the money supply will result in inflation, so any choice that refers to decreasing inflation may be eliminated.

339. (D) Choice (D) is correct. High cyclical unemployment indicates a recession, so the Federal Reserve might implement an expansionary fiscal policy.

340. (C) Choice (C) is correct. A rising price level could result in excessive inflation, which the Federal Reserve could fix by shrinking the money supply.

341. (C) Choice (C) is correct. The equation for the quantity theory of money includes the other four variables.

342. (A) Choice (A) is the best answer because monetary policy works quickly to increase or decrease aggregate demand as compared to the length of time it takes for the effects of taxes and government spending to be felt in the economy.

343. (B) Choice (B) is correct. A contractionary monetary policy is being implemented when securities are being sold. As a result, the lending power of a commercial bank decreases due to less money in the money supply.

344. (A) Choice (A) is correct. The discount rate refers to the interest rate the Fed sets for loans given out to commercial banks. As the rate is decreased, more commercial banks will seek loans from the Fed. If the Fed is selling government securities, then a contractionary monetary policy is being implemented, which results in a tighter money supply. It would therefore be counterproductive to lower the discount rate at the same time.

345. (E) Choice (E) is correct. If the economy is experiencing high unemployment and low economic growth, then it would be best to stimulate the economy to encourage growth. Therefore, the Fed should pursue an easy money policy and buy government securities.

346. (B) If the central bank is implementing a contractionary policy, then it is trying to combat inflation. One way to combat inflation is to decrease the supply of money.

347. (C) Choice (C) is correct. The discount rate refers to the interest rate the Fed sets to loans given out to commercial banks. As the rate is decreased, more commercial banks will seek loans from the Fed. This would help stimulate the economy.

348. (A) Choice (A) is the best answer because if the country is experiencing high unemployment, then one way monetary and fiscal policy could help is to increase aggregate demand by pursuing expansionary policies. So look for the answer that suggests buying government securities and increasing government spending.

349. (C) Choice (C) is correct. If the Fed is buying government securities, then it is pursuing an expansionary money policy, thus trying to stimulate the economy and economic growth. Buying securities increases the money supply—in this case by $50 million.

350. (A) An expansionary monetary policy seeks to increase aggregate demand. The major method the central bank has to implement this policy is buying government securities, which would increase the money supply and push the aggregate demand curve to the right.

351. (A) Demand-pull inflation refers to inflation caused by an increasing aggregate demand as it moves toward the upward sloping range of aggregate supply.

352. (A) Choice (A) is correct. Cost-push inflation deals with aggregate supply and an increase in price level due to an increase in the costs of production.

353. (A) Choice (A) is correct. If the economy is in a recession, then the government will attempt to stimulate aggregate demand through expansionary fiscal and monetary policies. If the economy is experiencing inflation, then the government will attempt to contract the money supply and bring the overall price level down.

354. (B) Choice (B) is correct. Built-in, or automatic, stabilizers are part of nondiscretionary fiscal policy, where no action is needed from the policy makers to make a change to government spending or borrowing.

355. (D) Choice (D) is correct. Built-in, or automatic, stabilizers are part of nondiscretionary fiscal policy, where no action is needed from the policy makers to make a change to government spending or borrowing.

356. (A) Choice (A) is the best answer because recognition lag is the delay in which an event or shock is felt or noticed by society. This may result in a lag in implementing counteracting monetary and fiscal policies.

357. (A) Choice (A) is correct. Built-in, or automatic, stabilizers are part of nondiscretionary fiscal policy, where no action is needed from the policy makers to make a change to government spending or borrowing.

358. (D) Choice (D) is correct. If the costs of production lead to an increase in the cost of a good or service without an increase in overall production, it is said to be cost-push inflation.

359. (C) Choice (C) is correct. The Federal Reserve System has three main tools: buying/selling securities, the discount rate, and the reserve ratio. These three tools are very powerful in implementing fast-acting monetary policy.

360. (A) Increasing the discount rate will discourage commercial banks from borrowing money from the central bank due to the increased costs of higher interest rates.

361. (A) Choice (A) is correct. The crowding out effect states that interest rates will rise due to increased government borrowing. The scenario in this question is a result of government borrowing. If the government chooses to increase borrowing to fund additional spending, this will result in crowding out private investors.

362. (C) Choice (C) is correct. Lowering the discount rate would encourage commercial banks to borrow more from the Fed, and money creation will increase.

363. (D) Choice (D) is correct. If the Fed lowered the reserve ratio, then the amount of money commercial banks are required to keep on reserve would decrease. This means there is more money to be lent out in the form of investments and loans.

364. (C) Choice (C) is correct. This is a basic definition of the velocity of money.

365. (A) Choice (A) is correct. Monetary policy does not include changes to taxation, infrastructure spending, transfer payments, and the Constitution.

366. (D) Choice (D) is correct. Lower taxes and more government spending would increase aggregate demand and supply.

367. (C) Reducing government spending is a contractionary fiscal policy.

368. (D) Choice (D) is correct. An expansionary fiscal policy would raise aggregate demand.

369. (C) Choice (C) is correct. The government can reduce inflation by raising taxes and reducing government spending. Increasing the reserve ratio would be monetary policy, which is controlled by the Federal Reserve.

370. (C) Choice (C) is correct. Higher government spending would cause demand-pull inflation, not lower government spending.

371. (B) Choice (B) is the best answer. If the money supply grows quickly, demand-pull inflation could result if the supply of goods does not grow rapidly as well.

372. (D) Choice (D) is correct. This would be an expansionary fiscal policy that could address cyclical unemployment caused by a recession.

373. (C) The increase in spending and a decrease in taxes would counteract each other, and the price level would not change.

374. (A) Choice (A) is correct. The MPS is 0.2 so the MPC must be 0.8. The multiplier would be $1/(1 - 0.8) = 5$ so $20 billion in government spending would increase aggregate demand by $100 billion.

375. (B) Choice (B) is correct. The MPS is 0.1 so the MPC must be 0.9. The multiplier would be $1/(1 - 0.9) = 10$ so reducing government spending by $5 billion would reduce aggregate demand by $50 billion.

376. (B) Choice (B) is correct. Aggregate demand would shift to the right because of the tax cut.

377. (C) Choice (C) is correct. Aggregate demand would shift to the left because of the reduction in spending.

378. (D) Choice (D) is correct. Corporate tax cuts would require legislation from the federal government, while the other four choices are examples of transfer payments that go into effect automatically.

379. (B) Choice (B) is the best answer. A high MPC results in a larger multiplier effect from the built-in stabilizer. Imports and high savings rates reduce the multiplier effect.

380. (B) The money supply would increase.

381. (A) Choice (A) is correct. A contractionary fiscal policy would reduce aggregate demand and weaken the dollar, increasing exports.

382. (D) Choice (D) is the best answer because an increase in government spending has a larger multiplier effect than a tax cut.

383. (C) A contractionary monetary policy would reduce aggregate demand.

384. (C) Choice (C) is correct. This is the definition of a recession.

385. (B) Choice (B) is the best answer. Decreasing the discount rate would be an expansionary monetary policy, and Choices (A), (C), and (D) are contractionary.

386. (D) Choice (D) is correct. The first three choices are fiscal policy.

387. (C) Choice (C) is correct. Contractionary monetary policy will reduce demand, so firms will employ fewer workers.

388. (D) Choice (D) is correct. The federal government controls fiscal policy, which includes setting federal tax rates.

389. (A) Choice (A) is correct. If central banks buy securities, the money supply increases and banks have more lending power.

390. (D) Choice (D) is correct. A tight money policy and selling government securities would reduce the money supply and limit inflation.

391. (B) Choice (B) is correct. The money supply would increase.

392. (B) Choice (B) is correct. A discount rate hike would reduce inflation and prevent the economy from overheating.

393. (B) Choice (B) is correct. Selling government securities reduces the money supply by the same amount.

394. (C) Choice (C) is the best answer. A tight money policy would reduce aggregate demand.

395. (C) Choice (C) is the best answer. A lower discount rate would increase the money supply, so commercial banks would have more lending power.

396. (D) Choice (D) is correct. Transfer payments would increase automatically, while the other choices would require legislation from Congress.

397. (B) Choice (B) is the best answer. A progressive income tax system acts as an automatic stabilizer because the average tax rate will drop during a recession.

398. (D) Choice (D) is the best answer. Health care subsidies are an automatic stabilizer because they increase when the economy weakens and incomes decrease.

399. (A) Choice (A) is the best answer. High interest rates encourage consumers to invest rather than holding onto cash, and vice versa.

400. (B) Choice (B) is the best answer. Reducing the size of the money supply would increase the velocity of the money in circulation.

401. (B) Choice (B) is correct. An increase in output or an increase in the price level will increase the velocity of money. An increase in the money supply will reduce the velocity of money.

402. (C) Choice (C) is correct. A decrease in the price level or an increase in money supply would both reduce the velocity of money.

403. (D) Choice (D) is correct. The velocity of money would be $900 million divided by $300 million, or 3.

404. (B) Choice (B) is correct. An increase in output would increase the velocity of money if the other two components of the equation $V = (P \times Q)/M$ did not change.

405. (B) Choice (B) is correct. GDP is equal to $(P \times Q)$ so GDP divided by the money supply is equal to the velocity of money.

406. (D) Choice (D) is correct. X / $300 million = 2 so X must be $600 million.

407. (E) Choice (E) is correct. If $600 million / X = 3, X must be $200 million.

408. (A) Choice (A) is correct. GDP would increase from $450 million to $600 million, a $150 million increase.

409. (C) Choice (C) is the best answer. If aggregate demand is at AD2 and a recession occurs, demand could shift to AD1. An automatic stabilizer could counteract the effects of the recession and shift demand back to AD2.

410. (C) Choice (C) is the best answer. Without an automatic stabilizer in place, aggregate demand would decrease, which would be represented by a shift to the left. While Choice (D) also represents a shift to the left, aggregate demand was not at AD3 before the recession.

411. (B) Choice (B) is correct. The Laffer curve shows a relationship between tax revenue and tax rates.

412. (D) Choice (D) is the best answer. The Laffer curve suggests that a tax cut will increase tax revenue if the tax rate is located on the right side of the curve. A tax cut will decrease tax revenue if the tax rate is located on the left side of the curve.

413. (A) Choice (A) is correct. Because of the crowding out effect, when the government borrows money from consumers the amount of loanable funds available to other borrowers decreases, so the supply of loanable funds shifts to the left.

414. (E) When the central bank sells bonds, it decreases the amount of currency in circulation. This—along with the government deficit spending—crowds out investment by demanding a greater supply of loanable funds, and this causes the SLF to shift left.

415. (A) Choice (A) is correct. Real GDP would increase by ($5 billion × 4), or $20 billion, increasing from $40 billion to $60 billion. This corresponds with a shift from AD2 to AD3. The price level would not change.

416. (C) Choice (C) is correct. Real GDP would decrease by ($20 billion × 2), or $40 billion, falling from $60 billion to $20 billion. This corresponds with a shift from AD3 to AD1. The price level would not change.

417. (B) Choice (B) is correct. An increase in government spending with aggregate supply in the classical region would increase the price level but wouldn't affect GDP.

418. (E) Choice (E) is correct. The economy is already at full employment at AD1, so any further increase in demand will keep the economy at full employment and increase prices.

419. (D) Choice (D) is correct. If the MPC is 0.5, the multiplier is $1/(1 - 0.5) = 2$ so increasing government spending by $10 billion would raise aggregate demand by $20 billion.

420. (B) Choice (B) is correct. If the MPC is 0.9, the multiplier is $1/(1 - 0.9) = 10$ so reducing government spending by $4 billion would raise aggregate demand by $40 billion.

421. (A) Per capita GDP represents the total output a country produces in a year divided by the total population. GDP can be calculated by adding up the population's income for the year. Choice (A) is the best answer because if per capita GDP increases, then it signals an increase in the standard of living for that country. Choice (B) is incorrect because a decrease in the standard of living would not coincide with an increase in per capita GDP. Choice (C) is incorrect because contractionary measures taken by the Fed are meant to decrease inflation. Choices (D) and (E) are incorrect because this would occur when the economy is in a downturn.

422. (E) Choice (E) is correct. You must know the definition of per capita GDP to answer this question. Per capita GDP represents the total output a country produces in a year divided by the total population.

423. (A) Choice (A) is the best answer because for an economy to increase its output without increasing any of the factors of production, new technologies must be utilized to increase output. Choices (B), (D), and (E) are incorrect because they refer to the factors of production. The question states economic growth without a change in the factors of production, so these choices should be eliminated immediately.

424. (E) Choice (E) is correct. Economics can compare living standards among countries by calculating per capita GDP, which is the total GDP divided by the total population. A high per capita GDP reflects a high standard of living, because one way to calculate GDP is to total the incomes in the country for the year.

425. (C) Choice (C) is correct. Human capital refers to the knowledge and skills a worker possesses. The worker contributes this knowledge and skills to the work that he or she does. Receiving education training for a job is an increase in human capital. Choice (A) is incorrect because it refers to the flow of investment on financial assets.

426. (A) Choice (A) is the best answer because it reflects the relationship between capital (a factor of production) and GDP: if one of the factors of production increases, GDP will increase along with wages. All other answers should be dismissed because they reflect a decrease or no change in GDP with an increase in capital stock.

427. (D) Choice (D) is the best answer because this idea reflects supply-side economics, where policies give tax breaks to the wealthy so they can take that money and invest, therefore creating an increase in production and economic growth. The investments will not pay off immediately, so this policy is designed to produce growth in the long term.

428. (B) Investment in technology, or capital, would increase the possible production and productive efficiency within the economy, allowing for future growth.

429. (C) Choice (C) is the best answer. A decrease in capital stock reduces the factors of production, resulting in lower GDP and lower wages.

430. (C) Choice (C) is the best answer. Increasing public education spending will result in a more skilled workforce, increasing the nation's human capital.

431. (A) Choice (A) is correct. Per capita GDP is total GDP divided by population.

432. (C) Choice (C) is correct. Population can be calculated by dividing total GDP by per capita GDP.

433. (A) Choice (A) is the best answer. An increase in per capita GDP does not indicate an increase in any specific GDP component, but it does indicate that the standard of living has increased.

434. (E) Choice (E) is correct. Per capita GDP does not provide information about any of the other factors mentioned here.

435. (A) To calculate per capita GDP, you must divide the amount of the increase by the total population within the country.

436. (C) Choice (C) is the best answer. The total GDP would be distributed across a larger population so per capita GDP would decrease.

437. (B) Choice (B) is correct. The increase in GDP would be distributed across the same population so per capita GDP and the standard of living would increase.

438. (C) The standard of living within a country is directly tied to the amount of production within a country. Therefore, if total GDP increases, it will cause an increase in the standard of living. The amount of the increase in standard of living will be in direct proportion to the increase in population.

439. (B) Choice (B) is correct. Per capita GDP is total GDP divided by population.

440. (D) Indonesia grew more rapidly than New Zealand because its per capita GDP increase was five times larger with no change in population.

Chapter 6: Open Economy—International Trade and Finance

441. (B) The import quota on cars will decrease the supply, causing an increase in the price in the market for cars.

442. (E) A capital account shows the flow of investment of real or financial assets between two nations. A balance of payment is a summary of payments received and sent between a nation and a foreign nation. The key to answering this question is to find the answer that has a relationship between two nations. Choice (E) is the only choice that reflects this dynamic.

443. (E) Choice (E) is the best answer because if the Australian economy is growing, then there is an increase in demand for U.S. goods, which increases the value of the U.S. dollar. The Australian dollar would depreciate.

444. (C) If interest rates rise, it will increase the cost of capital investment, causing it to decline. This will cause the rate of return on financial investments to rise, causing them to increase.

445. (D) Choice (D) is correct. A tariff is a tax placed on foreign goods as a way to protect domestic producers.

446. (D) Choice (D) is the best answer because even though the nation of XYZ produces bananas, if the world price is lower than the domestic price, a shortage is created. The nation of XYZ will import cheaper foreign bananas to correct the domestic shortage.

447. (B) Choice (B) is the best answer because it correctly defines a current account. A current account shows payments on imports and exports of goods and services and investment income sent abroad and received by the United States. Therefore, if there was a surplus in the current account, that means more investments from abroad came into the United States than export investments went out.

448. (A) Choice (A) is correct. A quota will increase the price of foreign imported rice. Consumers may start to buy other starches to substitute for rice.

449. (B) Choice (B) is the best answer because it is the only answer that illustrates the purpose of a tariff: a tax placed on foreign goods as a way to protect domestic producers.

450. (E) Choice (E) is correct. An import quota sets a maximum number of goods that can be imported into the domestic market. A quota does not collect revenue for the government.

451. (A) Choice (A) is the best answer because if a nation's currency depreciates, domestic goods become less expensive to foreign consumers.

452. (B) Choice (B) is correct. When a nation's currency falls or weakens in price relative to another currency, it has depreciated. In the case of this question, fewer U.S. dollars would be needed to buy Japanese yen.

453. (E) Choice (E) is correct. When a nation buys a foreign company, real estate, or the financial assets of another nation, these transactions appear in the capital account of the balance of payments statement.

454. (C) Choice (C) is correct. The law of comparative advantage states that countries benefit by trading goods they can produce at low opportunity costs for goods that would incur higher opportunity costs to produce.

455. (D) The law of comparative advantage states that countries benefit by trading goods they can produce at low opportunity costs for goods that would incur higher opportunity costs to produce. Choice (D) is the best answer because each country should produce its good at a lower opportunity cost than the other.

456. (A) The foreign exchange markets for currency are simply supply and demand markets that rely on other currency markets to determine movements of supply and demand.

457. (D) Choice (D) is correct. If the value of a nation's currency rises in relation to another nation's currency, it appreciated in value.

458. (A) Choice (A) is the best answer because a nation will always have a trade surplus if the number of exports is higher than the number of imports. Choice (B) is incorrect because it reflects a trade deficit. Choices (C) and (D) are incorrect because these forces would not ensure a trade surplus. Choice (E) is incorrect because if the U.S. dollar appreciates relative to another nation's currency, it would make U.S. goods more expensive and the number of exports would decrease.

459. (C) Choice (C) is correct. The answer to this question is very self-explanatory. Domestic prices are used for trade within a country, when there is no need to use world prices. When a country engages in trade with another country, world prices are used.

460. (D) Choice (D) is correct. The definition of capital account is the flow of investment on real or financial assets between a nation and foreigners. Choices (A) and (B) are incorrect because they refer to methods to protect domestic producers. Choice (C) is incorrect, although subtracting the current account from the capital account equals the balance of payments. Choice (E) is incorrect because it refers to setting the world price of goods.

461. (B) Choice (B) is the best answer because if a nation's currency appreciates (rises in value), more money is needed to purchase that nation's goods. This would result in a decrease in that nation's exports.

462. (B) Choice (B) is the best answer because nations choose to specialize and trade based on comparative advantage or low opportunity costs. Choices (A) and (C) are incorrect because they are negative arguments against NAFTA. Choice (E) is not related to the arguments supporting NAFTA.

463. (C) Choice (C) is correct. Choices (A) and (B) may be eliminated because they refer to economic organizations beyond the Western Hemisphere. Choice (D) is incorrect because it increased the severity of the Great Depression throughout the world. Choice (E) is incorrect because it was enacted in the 1930s, but the question is asking for economic integration in recent years. NAFTA began in 1994.

464. (A) The price of the dollar, or exchange rate, rising makes it more expensive for foreign travelers or exporters to the United States to buy dollars.

465. (B) The price of the dollar, or exchange rate, falling makes it less expensive for American travelers or importers from the United States to buy foreign currencies.

466. (E) Choice (E) is the best answer. The import quota makes fewer foreign goods available on the market, so domestic employers need to hire more employees to meet demand.

467. (B) Choice (B) is correct. A deficit in the balance of trade indicates that the country's imports exceed its exports.

468. (C) Choice (C) is the best answer. A stronger domestic currency would increase imports and reduce exports, widening the current account deficit.

469. (A) Choice (A) is the best answer. Reducing the discount rate would make borrowing money less costly for international investors, increasing foreign capital investment.

470. (C) Choice (C) is correct. The recession would reduce imports from Brazil, which would result in a stronger Mexican peso compared to the Brazilian real.

471. (C) Choice (C) is the best answer. The British pound would be weaker, so imports from Britain would be less expensive for Canadians.

472. (A) Choice (A) is correct. The low price of cheese in France indicates a surplus, which can be corrected by higher cheese exports.

473. (A) Choice (A) is correct. Removing the tariff would make domestic automobile manufacturers more vulnerable to foreign competition.

474. (C) Choice (C) is correct. The import quota would help the domestic sugar industry, but the amount of sugar purchased in the United States would decrease.

475. (B) Choice (B) is correct. Remittances are included in net factor income, a component of the current account.

476. (D) Choice (D) is correct. Removing the currency peg means that the currency can trade freely, so it was floated.

477. (C) Choice (C) is correct. When a currency has a fixed exchange value, it has a constant exchange rate in comparison to another currency.

478. (A) Choice (A) is the best answer. The tariff would protect inefficient Canadian lumber producers and removing it favors more efficient lumber companies.

479. (B) Choice (B) is the best answer. The transaction would be an outflow of foreign assets recorded in the capital account.

480. (C) Choice (C) is the best answer. A nation has other options besides tariffs and quotas if it wants to protect domestic firms.

481. (B) Choice (B) is the best answer. Dumping occurs when an exporter sells goods below cost to damage domestic producers.

482. (C) Choice (C) is the best answer. Free trade would not stop dumping, but the other options would penalize the exporter.

483. (B) Choice (B) is correct. The dollar buys $90/60 = 1.5$ times as many rupees as before, so it appreciated 50 percent.

484. (A) Choice (A) is correct. The dollar buys $10/20 = 0.5$ times as many pesos as before, so it depreciated 50 percent.

485. (C) Choice (C) is correct. A strong dollar policy would make imports less expensive.

486. (B) Choice (B) is correct. The weaker dollar would make the U.S. more attractive for international tourists.

487. (E) Choice (E) is correct. The discount rate didn't change, so the cost of imports wouldn't change either.

488. (D) Choice (D) is correct. A weak dollar helps domestic exporters.

489. (B) Choice (B) is correct. When a central bank raises the discount rate, the currency it issues will increase in value.

490. (E) Choice (E) is correct. Both central bank decisions strengthen the U.S. dollar against the Canadian dollar and Canada will export more goods and services to America.

491. (B) Choice (B) is correct. Americans would sell dollars and buy reals to pay for Brazilian sugar.

492. (C) Choice (C) is the best answer. Inflation will cause a currency to lose value against foreign currencies.

493. (C) Choice (C) is correct. The tariff is a tax so the French government would collect more tax revenue.

494. (A) Choice (A) is the best answer. Expectations would cause the value of the New Zealand dollar to rise, increasing imports and decreasing exports.

495. (C) Choice (C) is the best answer. The increased supply will depreciate the Norwegian kroner.

496. (B) Choice (B) is the best answer. Increased demand will cause the Russian ruble to appreciate.

497. (B) Choice (B) is correct. A limit on the quantity of imported goods is a quota.

498. (B) Choice (B) is correct. The treaty would be a free trade agreement.

499. (B) Choice (B) is correct. The yen buys $150/100 = 1.5$ times as many dollars as it did before, so it appreciated 50 percent against the dollar.

500. (A) Choice (A) is correct. The Brazilian real buys $3/6 = 0.5$ times as many dollars as it did before, so it depreciated 50 percent against the dollar.